The
Age of Metternich
1814-1848

REVISED EDITION

. . .

Arthur J. May

University of Rochester

THE DRYDEN PRESS
Hinsdale, Illinois

Preface

Except for the title, the broad pattern of organization, and an occasional sentence or two, this revision differs radically from the original edition. Longer perspective, deeper knowledge, and new viewpoints have compelled thorough overhauling.

Metternich and other hardened upholders of the status quo, for instance, appear in a less odious light to a generation that has witnessed a surfeit of wicked, charismatic, totalitarian dictators in Europe. To have lived, moreover, through the storms and stresses of two world-wide wars renders the historian automatically immune to the facile optimism of continuous human progress that captivated many an intellectual as the nineteenth century moved along. Not least, Russia and European economic affairs are awarded much fuller attention than in the first edition.

This work presents a short reconstruction of Continental Europe between the first abdication of Napoleon and the violent hurricane of 1848. Running through the entire period were the impact of English institutions and manners of life, the epochal aspirations of the great French Revolution, and a new technology, symbolized by the steam-powered machine and steam transport. Wealth and health improved; clashing purposes tended to separate the traditionally privileged strata from the ambitious bourgeoisie, and the latter element in turn from the growing class of urban workpeople, many of them huddled together in sprawling, unsanitary environments. Gathering force decade after decade, machine industrialism wrought profoundly upon nearly every phase of life and thought.

Or that at least was the general panorama north of the Pyrenees and for a short stretch east of the Rhine. By the 1830s, too, the United States had begun to loom up as the dream country for the poor of western Europe. To the east of the Continent, the Hapsburg Empire notably, and more so the realm of the Romanovs, seemed relatively invulnerable to fermenting novelties.

Volatile and excitable Paris, contrasting strongly with the phlegmatic French countryside, set the pace for the eternal flow of change in European politics and economics.

In the absence of effective constitutional instruments of law, secret societies and plottings as well as the knife and the bullet were invoked against misgovernment, tyranny, and denial of nationhood or for broadening the area of freedom. Chiefly, middle-class men furnished the leadership, yet few of them found conspiracy so engrossing as to interfere with the day-by-day task of earning their daily bread. Officials of state, on their part, faced the continuous challenge of coping with the unexpected in the world of affairs.

For mature men of 1814—as for ourselves—the future stretched ahead like an uncharted ocean, full of uncertainties and the mystery of the unknown. Yet the concern of the European man was not restricted to political and economic affairs. To understand him, it is essential to know of his curiosity about the eternal verities, his varied approaches to the overarching riddles of the good life, his achievements in literature and the arts. These fundamental matters are surveyed in the final chapter.

Properly interpreted, history is in a peculiar sense a fruitful corrective to highly specialized study. It is expected of the historian (or ought to be) that he excite questions and then direct the curious person to books where answers may be discovered. "A Bibliographical Note" reads the caption over the final section of this work, which contains a selection of first-rate writings illuminating the "Age of Metternich."

The reader should have an atlas close at hand for easy reference. Recommended are Edward W. Fox, Ed., *Atlas of European History* (New York, 1957), pages 41 and 44, or F. W. Putzger, Ed., *Historischer Atlas* (Berlin, 1961), pages 96, 98, 99, 102, and 105.

It is a pleasure to record my deep gratitude to Mrs. Margie Redmond of Rochester for her skill and patience in converting my tangled long-hand pages into neat typescript.

The University of Rochester   A. J. M.
1963

Contents

Preface v

1 **The Congress of Vienna and its Aftermath**   **1**

Prince Clemens von Metternich   *1*
The Ideas and Character of a Prince   *3*
The First French Settlement   *5*
Men and Methods at Vienna   *7*
Quarrels Among the Peacemakers   *11*
The Hundred Days   *12*
Second Treaty of Paris   *13*
A New Europe   *14*
Minor Agreements   *18*
An Adventure in Cooperation   *18*
The Birth of the Monroe Doctrine   *24*
Summary   *25*

2 **Convalescence and Convulsions**   **27**

The French Restoration   *27*
Troubles in the Iberian Peninsula   *30*
Ferment in Italy   *33*
Risings in 1820–1821   *38*
The Evolution of Germany   *39*
Turk and Serb   *45*
The Winning of Greek Independence   *47*
The Empire of the Tsars   *51*
The Reign of Alexander I   *55*
Episode in December   *58*
The Passing of the Bourbons   *60*
Summary   *62*

3   The Gathering Storm   *64*

A July Kingdom Comes   *64*
Independent Belgium   *68*
Ferment in Italy   *69*
The Course of German History   *72*
The Hapsburg Realm   *78*
Hapsburg Peoples   *80*
An Era Ends   *85*
The "Iron" Tsardom   *87*
The Eastern Riddle   *94*
The July Monarchy—Last Phase   *97*
Novel Social Doctrines   *99*
A New Revolution   *103*
Summary   *104*

4   The Harvest of Culture   *106*

The Catholic Church   *106*
Protestantism and Its Thinkers   *111*
Biblical Studies   *113*
Orthodox Eastern Christianity   *114*
The State of Jewry   *117*
European Literature   *118*
Romanticist Poetry   *119*
Slavic Literature   *121*
Romantic Drama   *122*
Novels of the Romantic Era   *123*
The Loom of History   *126*
Romanticism in the Fine Arts   *129*
Architecture   *132*
Music   *135*
The Large Picture   *139*

Bibliographical Note   *140*

Index   *149*

C H A P T E R . . . 1

The Congress of Vienna and Its Aftermath

Prince Clemens von Metternich

Whether men shape the course of human affairs or events mold the careers of men, has long been debated. Certain students of society, such as the Concord sage Ralph Waldo Emerson, believe that "an institution is the lengthened shadow of one man, and all history resolves itself very easily into the biographies of a few stout and earnest persons." But Karl Marx, the leading nineteenth-century philosopher of anticapitalism, argued that economic forces really determine all facets of the human pageant. Between the extremes of Emerson and Marx exists a wide variety of shades of interpretation.

In any case, there is appropriateness in thinking of the evolution of Continental Europe between the first abdication of Napoleon and the revolutionary upheavals of 1848 as the "Age of Metternich." For almost all of those thirty-four years, the Austrian prince loomed large on the international stage, and a philosophy of government espoused by him held sway over most of Europe.

Born at Coblentz in the Rhineland in 1773, Metternich belonged to a family of landed aristocrats, and an aristocrat he remained to the day of his death. By the standards of the time he was well educated, attending lectures at the universities of Strasbourg and Mainz. In educational experience he was more the Frenchman than a German; and of the five languages with which he was familiar, he preferred French most of all. Somewhere along the line he developed interest in a broad range of cultural and intellectual matters that he cultivated fitfully through a long and busy public life. When the armies of revolutionary France swept into the Rhineland, the Metternich properties were seized, and the impoverished family wandered off to Vienna, there to take employment in the diplomatic service of the venerable House of Hapsburg.

Charming, urbane, and affable—lucky too—Metternich married the granddaughter of Count Wenzel von Kaunitz, long the trusted counsellor of the Austrian imperial family. That union, together with an inborn flair for the diplomatic art, enabled Metternich to move rapidly up the diplomatic ladder. At the age of thirty-three, four years the junior of Napoleon, he was appointed ambassador to the imperial court in Paris. The strengths and weaknesses of Bonaparte he appraised with remarkable accuracy. Becoming Austrian foreign minister in 1809, he consolidated his standing with the French emperor by promoting the emperor's marriage to a Hapsburg archduchess, Marie Louise.

When the 1812 Bonapartist campaign against Russia turned out disastrously, Metternich, now a prince, hastened to organize a European coalition which managed to defeat the French armies. With Napoleon shipped off to the island of Elba, the Austrian prince occupied a commanding position in Europe, and he undertook to secure the application of principles which he considered necessary if the Old World were to enjoy the grandest of all blessings: peace, both internationally and inside the European states.

"Few men have understood me," the prince once soliloquized; "writers a hundred years hence will judge me very differently from those of today." Contemporaries who cared about civil liberties, about constitutions providing for parliamentary government and manhood participation in it, or those who wished to see Germans, Italians, and smaller nationalities united in independent, national states, bitterly assailed Metternich as a tyrant, a black ogre, and a pitiless reactionary. These adversaries, who in the context of their time may be called liberals,

> "Would grasp Metternich until
> I feel his cold red throat distil
> In blood through these two hands."

That interpretation was perpetuated by historical writers who looked upon the past through the lenses of liberalism, as defined above.

The Ideas and Character of a Prince

Metternich abhorred "liberalism" as the mainspring of the torments and bloodshed which revolutionary France had visited upon mankind. To his way of thinking, aspirations for popular government, civil freedoms, and the like were a dread disease that had captured vocal elements among the middle classes—business and professional men, professors and other workers in ideas. They were troublemakers who had to be watched, restrained and if necessary repressed by physical force. The mind of Metternich was everlastingly haunted by the specter of a vast conspiracy aiming at the destruction of the prevailing governmental and social order.

Along with other like-minded public personalities, the Austrian prince believed that the mass of Europeans yearned for security, quiet, and peace, and regarded liberal abstractions as repugnant or were utterly in-

different to them. The best of all patterns of government, he insisted, was autocratic absolutism, upheld by
a loyal army, by a submissive, decently efficient bureaucratic and police machine, and by trustworthy churchmen. This creed and variants Metternich set out in
lengthy state papers and letters.

For all his attachment to the methods of authoritarianism, he detected much that was praiseworthy in
the British parliamentary system, and he viewed with
tolerance the constitutional regimes in France, in several of the south German states, and in Hungary.
Though he struck sharply at political novelties and
deviations, he was too close in spirit to Voltaire to be a
tyrant; compared with an Adolf Hitler or a Joseph
Stalin, Metternich was mild and humane.

By experience and inclination a cosmopolitan, the
Rhineland expatriate envisioned a stable, cooperative
Europe resting on preservation of the status quo and a
balance of physical strength between the major powers.
"Europe has for a long time," he remarked in 1824 to
the Duke of Wellington, "held for me the significance
of a fatherland." Up to a point that confession rang
true, but it seems fair to say that transcending this
allegiance to the "European idea" was his determination to advance the international prestige of and to
ensure internal discipline in his adopted Austria. For
the integrity of this multinationality realm, the prince
understood, political innovations in neighboring areas
would need to be prevented and national aspirations,
especially among Germans and Italians, denied.

Astute, sharp-witted, sophisticated, Metternich contributed significantly to the settlements at the end of
the Napoleonic warfare and exerted great influence
upon the high politics of Europe for thirty years longer.
At every turn, of course, his conduct of policy was
somewhat shaped by conditions inside Austria—its
military resources, the state of its public finances, the
stability of its government.

In maturity, Metternich was an amiable and polished

grand seigneur, living on grants from the Austrian treasury or on loans furnished by the Rothschilds or some other banking house. As painted by the fashionable English portraitist, Sir Thomas Lawrence, Metternich in his prime was of medium height and slender shoulders, and he had an abnormally large chest. His hair was curly, his eyes blue, his mouth large, his nose beaklike, his brow prominent, and his hands long and thin. Acquaintances remarked upon his dignified appearance and his harsh, squeaky voice.

The Austrian prince built up a legendary reputation for diplomatic finesse and devotion to public duty. It was not a case, however, of all work and no play, for he delighted in parties and he was fond of ladies, invariably selecting his mistresses from the socially elite. Dramatically alive women were in fact his sole lifelong enthusiasm. Except for a few university professors and physicians, he restricted his associations to the aristocracy.

Easily flattered, Metternich was an extremely conceited man. "Error never had access to my mind," he boasted even after a revolutionary storm had driven him from power. Conceiving of himself as a "rock against which the waves of disorder beat in vain" in a turbulent generation, he remarked that "the behavior of people toward me is rather that of sponges, anxious to absorb ideas. . . ." A German author devoted an entire book to the vanity of Metternich!

The First French Settlement

Napoleon had turned Europe upside down. In 1814, his grand design—an empire larger than Charlemagne's though less extensive than Hitler's, extended from Gibraltar to the Vistula River—lay in ruins. Statesmen of the victorious Allied coalition undertook the task of reordering the Continent in two stages. First, a peace settlement was arranged with France, and then the pacification of the rest of Europe and to a slight extent

of the wider world was prepared at a conference in
Vienna.

By the Treaty of Paris, May 1814, the boundaries of
France were fixed at the limits they had reached in
1792, and French colonies, with minor exceptions, were
handed back. No financial indemnity was exacted, and
France was not even required to return art treasures
removed from conquered countries. The settlement, in
short, was unusually lenient, and not likely to nourish
a spirit of vengeance. France remained great and powerful, and that was a real asset for the new government
imposed on the country by the Allied victors. It was
specified in the treaty that decisions on Europe outside
of France would be made at a general congress to con-
vene in the autumn of 1814.

With the blessing of the Allies, the legitimate Bourbon claimant to the throne of France, Louis XVIII,
brother of the last king, became king. Ravaged by
elephantiasis, the new ruler beat his way from England
to Paris. Having learned something as an exile, he
promised to reign as a constitutional monarch and he
forthwith published the Charter of 1814. This document reflected somewhat the transformation that had
come over France since the outbreak of the revolutionary storms, and had many similarities with the "un-
written" British constitution.

The charter contained a clear statement of the fundamental rights that all citizens possessed, such as freedom
of religion and expression, and equality before the law.
Executive authority, including the selection of ministers
was assigned to the crown. A lawmaking body of two
houses would be chosen on terms which virtually assured a controlling voice to the landed proprietors.
While members of the upper chamber would be picked
by the king, deputies in the lower house would be
elected by citizens who paid large direct taxes. To this
house was assigned the rights of originating money bills
and of impeaching the ministry, though on this latter
point the charter lacked precision. A clause in the

document confirmed the drastic changes in landholding that had come to pass during the Revolution. With small modifications, the Charter of 1814 remained in force for thirty-four years.

Upon the Bourbon Restoration, privileged French classes which had been in exile streamed back to their homeland. Spokesmen of the nobility pressed for compensation for land taken away from their class during the Revolution. Militant ecclesiastics clamored for the restoration of some of the privileges Roman Catholicism had possessed before 1789. A harsh fate, priests thundered from pulpits, would befall families who had acquired church lands and refused to hand them back.

Agitation by aristocrat and churchman provoked apprehension among small farmers and middle-class individuals of a liberal cast of mind. In military circles the belief prevailed that French prestige in the family of nations would be rehabilitated if Napoleon, the conqueror who had made himself Caesar, returned to power. The bitter memory of foreign occupation of Paris, unexampled since the day of Joan of Arc, could be erased. News of the gathering discontent reached the "little Corsican," exiled on the small island of Elba off the coast of Italy.

Men and Methods at Vienna

In September 1814, European statecraft converged upon the Hapsburg capital, Vienna, to define boundaries, choose rulers for several states, and hammer out understandings on lesser matters of international concern. It was fondly imagined that territorial issues could be quickly ironed out, and it was even supposed in some quarters that an international court of justice would be created and plans to limit armaments devised. In fact, however, diplomatic deliberations, often marked by sharp cleavages among the peacemakers, dragged on nearly nine months.

A community of nearly 300,000 at the time, Vienna

exercised a magnetic attraction upon crowned heads, pleasure-seeking aristocrats, and the choicest of courtesans, who came to intrigue, to enflame desires, and to entertain. Visiting royalty were lodged in the Hofburg, a vast pile of buildings in the heart of the Danubian capital that served as the principal imperial residence. For the diversion of the multitude of guests there was an unending chain of festivities—receptions and masquerades, dinners and sleighing parties, concerts and balls and more balls. After the prolonged ordeal of the Napoleonic nightmare, European top society felt it deserved a season of fun and frolic—and that it had. The Congress "danced," observed a wit with less than full accuracy; never had old Vienna been so animated or so gay, though taxpayers angrily protested that they had to foot bills in peacetime as heavy as those in war.

Across the way from the Hofburg in the baroque Ballhaus the real business of peacemaking was transacted. As a sign of equality between the five leading countries, five doors led into the central conference chamber, so that representatives might enter simultaneously. Conversations were conducted in the utmost privacy, but espionage flourished so that each major delegation was rather well aware of the designs and secrets of the others. The papers of the foremost negotiators and the reports of technical committees supply the most reliable information on what actually happened around the diplomatic table.

The real congress at Vienna amounted to the confidential exchanges within a committee of five, representing the larger powers allied against Napoleon and the chief delegate of the restored Bourbons of France. Ministers and agents of the smaller countries had precious little voice on the big questions of the day. Prince Metternich, a year younger than John F. Kennedy when he was inaugurated President of the United States, and the self-styled "coachman of Europe," acted as chairman, planner-in-chief, and master of ceremonies. His fixed goals entailed a settlement that promised to afford Europe security and peace and not only to safeguard, but indeed to enhance, the position of the House of Hapsburg. At the elbow of Metternich sat his confidant, Friedrich von Gentz (1764–1832), secretary of the policymaking band of five, a publicist by trade, a little mouse of a man, whose political outlook was even more conservative than that of his chief.

Championing the ambitions of Prussia was her second-rate king, Friederich William III, who entrusted actual negotiations to his elderly and profligate first minister, Prince Karl A. von Hardenberg (1750–1822), reputedly a progressive since he had carried out far-reaching social and political reforms at home. For the Prussian team the supreme territorial ambition was the acquisition of Saxony, whose king had injudiciously allied with Napoleon.

From Britain came Lord Castlereagh (and during his absence in London, the Duke of Wellington), a hard-headed and hard-working professional diplomatist who had exerted his admittedly extraordinary abilities to break the Napoleonic stranglehold on the Continent and who hated French revolutionary doctrines with pathological hatred. Faithful to the dogma of a balance of power on the Continent—the "just equilibrium" was his phrase for it—Castlereagh stubbornly and resourcefully opposed too great a territorial expansion by Russia, whose military might had been so convincingly demonstrated during the titanic struggle with France. On this point, and on others, the Briton saw eye to eye with Metternich whom he knew quite well.

Evidently the most glamorous personality in the galaxy of Vienna peacemakers was the tall, handsome, thirty-seven-year-old Alexander I, tsar of all the Russias "by the grace of the Almighty." Enigmatic, mercurial, yet altogether fascinating, he had been tagged in his youth a dangerous revolutionary. For him the closing stages in the warfare against the French had taken on the quality of a crusade, and he liked to think of himself as the liberator of Europe from the giant vampire —the little Corsican.

In the course of the eighteenth century, the empire

of the tsars, which previously had counted for little in
the high politics of Europe, had advanced to the rank
of a great power. Stolid, sturdy Muscovite soldiers had
helped greatly in delivering the *coup de grace* against
Napoleon. By 1814, the prestige of Russia, personified
by the tsar, had soared to a level it was not again to
approach until the close of the Second World War.
Inspired by the success of Russian armies in expelling
the Corsican demigod from their homeland, a British
poet exulted in 1813:

"Rise, children of Europe, march fearlessly forth,
    The pole star of liberty beams from the North,
    Be vengeance your cry, Alexander your trust,
    And tyranny's scepter shall crumble to dust."

Before the Congress of Vienna met and while it was
in progress, Alexander spoke in idealistic accents of the
brighter and more secure Europe that would emerge.
Yet, for all his melodious rhetoric, he was determined
to advance Russian national interests. Specifically, he
claimed a much larger share of Polish territory, which
was in fact occupied by his armies, than had belonged
to Russia after Poland had been partitioned late in the
eighteenth century. As an earnest of his "liberalism,"
Alexander talked of giving Russian Poland a constitution and a parliamentary form of government—and in
fact eventually did just that. Repeatedly he clashed
with Metternich and at one juncture challenged him
to a duel which the urbane Austrian prince turned
aside as indecent. But by the time the conference
ended, differences had been superficially smoothed
over, though hardly more than that, until 1818 when
political intimacy between autocrat and aristocrat deep-
ened and lasted throughout the rest of Alexander's reign.

Last but not least of the main peacemakers of 1814
was the foreign minister of Louis XVIII of France,
Charles M. de Talleyrand, ex-churchman, ex-henchman
of Bonaparte, whose talent for ingratiating himself
with the controlling power group in France was simply
amazing. His remarkable intelligence matched his natu-

ral arrogance. He was burdened with few illusions, fewer doctrines, and no scruples, save what were needed for survival. Since the Treaty of Paris had already arranged peace with France, this political chameleon and slick diplomatist could pose at Vienna as an "honest broker" on controversial questions. Priding himself on being the oracle of "the sacred principle of legitimacy," he lined up with pacific Britain and Austria. During one crisis, his silken tongue effectively developed the argument that the ambitions of Alexander I imperiled the future peace of Europe as Napoleon had done previously. It is a gross distortion to suppose, however, as one enthusiast has written "that the history of the conference is the history of Talleyrand's skillful diplomacy."

Quarrels among the Peacemakers

Following the First and Second World Wars, coalitions which were formed to defeat a common enemy experienced rough sledding, to speak modestly, in working out treaty settlements, once hostilities had ceased. It was thus also after Napoleon had been humbled. Divergent national interests, which seemed insurmountable, threatened to disrupt the Vienna meeting and precipitate a new war. Russian demands for Polish-inhabited territory paralleled the pretensions of the Prussians to the kingdom of Saxony. British and Austrian diplomacy intransigently resisted these claims, and Talleyrand and spokesmen of several small German states sided with it. Unless Alexander moderated his ambitions, Castlereagh warned, "the peace which we have so dearly purchased will be of short duration."

Indeed, feuding turned so violent that Talleyrand, Metternich, and Castlereagh signed on January 3, 1815, a secret alliance pointed against the Russo-Prussian combination. It was intended to thwart the annexationist designs by arms if necessary. The three allies mobilized powerful armies, and in the face of the dissension at Vienna, Britain hastened to conclude a settlement with the United States, ending the War of 1812.

Whether Alexander actually learned of the tripartite understanding remains uncertain. Be that as it may, the tsar lowered his Polish demands, and the Prussian puppets dutifully followed suit. Whatever danger of war there may have been, evaporated, but before a compromise settlement had been fully fashioned a fresh peril arose: Napoleon had escaped from Elba and returned to France. Straightaway, Europe presented a united front against this new challenge by the once invincible Corsican.

The Hundred Days

Informed alike of the growing dissatisfaction in France with the Bourbon restoration and of the disputes at Vienna, Bonaparte resolved to seek the French throne again. Upon landing on the Continent, he prophetically proclaimed, "The eagle with the national colors will fly from steeple to steeple till it reaches the tower of Notre Dame." Ordered by Louis XVIII to apprehend Bonaparte, Marshal Michel Ney, promised to bring him "back in an iron cage." But when his soldiers saw Napoleon, they shouted "Vive l'Empereur" and defected; the Marshal, known as the "bravest of the brave," likewise turned his coat. The progress to Paris was an immense personal triumph for Bonaparte; hardened army veterans, townsmen, and peasants rallied enthusiastically under the banner of the "Corsican corporal."

By decrees attuned to widespread popular wishes and by masterly patriotic appeals, nearly all of France was persuaded to uphold the emperor. A large army was quickly whipped into shape and ordered to march into Belgium to meet the advancing forces of the grand alliance. At Waterloo, in June 1815, after days of bloody fighting, the French forces suffered irretrievable defeat. Russian troops had no part in the Waterloo victory, though they were mobilized in the Rhineland ready to fight. Upon his second abdication, a British warship carried Bonaparte far away from Europe, to the South Atlantic island of St. Helena. There he spent the last six years of his spectacular career fancifully embroidering the epic Napoleonic legend.

Second Treaty of Paris

With Bonaparte out of the way, the Allies rode triumphantly into Paris again. Louis XVIII returned to the throne and resumed a course of prudence and moderation. Incensed by the popular ardor shown for the former emperor, Allied statecraft imposed a more severe treaty in November 1815, and exacted guarantees for pacific French behavior in the future. Breathing fire and flame, Prussian diplomacy, recalling how Napoleon had once conquered and occupied the patrimony of Frederick the Great, demanded that France be plundered and dismembered, but the other victors responded negatively.

Territory on the east, containing a population of half a million and embracing the Saar Valley, was cut away, but claims of the German powers to predominantly German-speaking Alsace-Lorraine were rejected by the other allies. A fairly large reparations bill was saddled upon France to be liquidated within five years; until the obligation was paid, Allied soldiers, Russians included, would occupy sections of France at French expense. Art objects that the French had stolen had now to be sent back to their rightful owners. France was being punished, plainly enough, but she had not been denied a position of influence among the powers. The second Bourbon Restoration had not been made unpopular by the exaction of drastic penalties. Compared with the settlement meted out to the defeated Central Empires after the First World War, for instance, France received remarkably magnanimous and far-sighted treatment.

A New Europe

Before Waterloo had been fought and won, the Allied statesmen at Vienna signed a "Final Act." In arriving at decisions on territory and rulers, several basic considerations guided in a general way the peacemakers. Secret wartime treaties for one, the determination to create a fairly strong circle of states around explosive France for another, and also doctrines of "legitimacy" and "compensation." In some states, the legitimate sovereigns were restored to thrones from which the French had ousted them; and in some instances, states obtained suitable compensation for territory they had lost.

As an example of the application of that last principle, Austria acquired the choice north Italian provinces of Lombardy[1] and Venetia and the Adriatic district of Dalmatia in compensation for the loss of the southern Netherlands, or Belgium. Thanks to these gains and others noted below, Austria emerged as second in population only to Russia among European states, and throughout the central section of the Continent from the Baltic to the Mediterranean, the voice of Austria was paramount in the sphere of politics. In the judgment of Castlereagh, a robust Hapsburg empire was an essential condition for peace and stability, or, in his own language, "the great hinge upon which the fate of Europe must ultimately depend."

Though Prussia was obliged to relinquish part of her former Polish holdings to Russia, it retained a considerable slice and added the harbor community of Danzig (Polish Gdańsk after the Second World War) and a strip of former Swedish land along the Baltic Sea. There was more, for Prussia picked up about two-fifths of potentially prosperous Saxony and made even more valuable acquisitions in the Rhineland. In keeping with the wish of Britain to have a strong state facing

---

[1] Strictly speaking, Lombardy was simply returned, having been under the rule of Austria throughout most of the eighteenth century (1714).

France, Prussia was awarded the Rhine valley from the Dutch frontier south to Coblentz. This area included Cologne and other historic communities and the Ruhr and most of the Saar valleys, one day to grow into thriving industrial districts. Altogether, Prussia, now a kingdom of about ten millions, came out of the Napoleonic agony very well indeed.

What remained of Saxony constituted a buffer state along the rim of the Austrian empire. In exchange for the Tyrol and lesser parcels handed back to Austria by special arrangement, Bavaria gained sovereignty over a section of the southern Rhineland. The grand duchy of Luxemburg became an independent state, politically associated with the crown of the Netherlands.

The dream of a united Germany, cherished by patriotic spirits, especially in educated circles, found no favor among the decision makers of Vienna. During the preceding generation the ancient and long moribund Holy Roman Empire of the German nation, under the headship of Austria, had been laid in a tomb, and many small German principalities had been merged into larger political units. The Vienna Congress instituted a community of the thirty-nine independent German states as the Germanic Confederation. This union, it was urged, would prevent small principalities from gravitating into the French orbit and would help to ensure peace in central Europe. It was prescribed that each state should issue a constitution with provisions for a representative assembly.

By assigning to Austria the presidency of the Confederation, the Vienna settlement confirmed the traditional ascendancy of the Danubian empire in German politics, though the Austrian emperor was no more than "first among equals." Representatives of the member-states would attend a federal diet, a pale version of a parliament, meeting at Frankfurt-am-Main. Since decisions in the diet on any proposition of substance required unanimous consent, the Confederation never achieved much significance as an instrument of government; yet it lingered on for half a century, until, that is, the assertive kingdom of Prussia built the German Empire on the ruins of the 1815 institution.

Though Alexander I was thwarted in his full ambition concerning Poland, Russia obtained the bear's share of that mutilated land, including Warsaw and adjoining districts formerly under the flag of Prussia. These annexations extended the long arm of the tsars well into central Europe, and, as other trophies of war, the Russian empire had taken Finland from Sweden in 1809, and Bessarabia from Turkey in 1812. Austria recovered the province of Galicia, which was inhabited by a mixture of Poles and Ukrainians (Ruthenians), save for Cracow, the medieval capital and holy of holies of the Polish nation. There an independent republic was set up, which lasted to 1846.

Ever since the collapse of the Roman Empire, the Italian peninsula had been politically disunited, and that melancholy situation was perpetuated by the peacemakers of 1814–1815. It was the rooted conviction of Metternich, who cynically though not inaccurately alluded to Italy as "a geographical expression," that the idea of a politically consolidated peninsula was a pipe dream of starry-eyed romantics. Castlereagh echoed this sentiment. Running from north to south, Lombardy and Venetia, as has been indicated, passed as a joint kingdom to Austria, Hapsburgs were installed as sovereigns in Tuscany and smaller north central duchies, and Hapsburg influence was appreciable in the States of the Church, the papal patrimony, reaching from Rome straight across the peninsula from sea to sea.

In the far south of Italy, the legitimate Bourbon claimant was restored to the kingship of the Two Sicilies with his capital at Naples; Austrian garrisons were maintained until 1818 in this largest of Italian states. Off to the northwest, the small kingdom of Sardinia (Piedmont), which was destined to serve as the nucleus around which a united Italy would one day take shape, gained the historic and commercially valuable Republic of Genoa. That arrangement, together with the powerful position of Austria in the peninsula, seemed to remove the likelihood of an attempt by France to interfere in the destinies of Italy.

As in France, so in Spain and Portugal the legitimate dynasties were reinstated. The peacemakers assigned to Switzerland a small portion of France, containing the city of Geneva, and recognizing the Alpine republic as a perpetually neutral country.

Quite in harmony with the principle of creating a *cordon sanitaire* around the French peace-disturber, Belgium, previously Austrian, was combined with Holland to form the kingdom of the Netherlands. This merger compensated the Dutch for colonies which Britain had snatched away. Farther to the north Norway was detached from Denmark, ending a union centuries old, and transferred to Sweden, whose ruler, Bernadotte, once a French marshal, had switched his resources to the anti-Bonapartist coalition at an opportune moment. Under the terms of this union, which persisted until dissolved peacefully in 1905, Norway possessed a broad measure of home rule.

Altogether, then, the diplomatists at Vienna had rearranged the map of Europe, west to east and north to south in a radical fashion. No sophisticated observer imagined, however, that the millennium would emerge from the building of this new Europe. The march of history, moreover, would stamp the term "impermanent" on nearly every part of the settlements.

In the tangible language of territory, how did Britain, most resourceful and tenacious adversary of Napoleon, profit from the general pacification? It was content with overseas acquisitions, colonies and islands having strategic or commercial potentialities. Off the mouth of the German Elbe River, for example, Britain took Heligoland from the Danes, and it reinforced its command of the Mediterranean by annexing Malta and the Greek-peopled Ionian Islands. From the Dutch, Britain wrested away Ceylon and the valuable Cape of Good Hope, the forerunner of the present republic of South Africa. France and Spain ceded islets which the

London ministry regarded as needful for the security of the globe-girdling British realm. Since the British fleet was the unchallenged mistress of the sea and since British diplomacy had accomplished what seemed essential for a stable and tranquil Continent, Britons could view with no little satisfaction the outcome of the harrowing duel with Bonaparte.

Minor Agreements

Into the Final Act of Vienna were woven several interesting international engagements of secondary significance. It was agreed, for one thing, that commerce along rivers traversing more than one European state should be encouraged by enlightened police and toll policies. Less effective was a proposal to stop the loathsome traffic in African slaves. British humanitarians pressed Castlereagh to secure a general accord to abolish the slave trade, comparable to legislation that had been enacted by Britain and the United States. But Continental powers with colonial holdings refused to approve the British initiative. All that could be secured was a declaration condemning the traffic in slaves and promising its cessation in the near future.

In a few years, the European powers adopted abolition measures, though only Britain faithfully enforced the laws, and a good deal of trading in black men persisted. Actually, it was not until 1890 that the transportation of slaves was prohibited by general agreement among the nations. Slavery itself had been abolished in French overseas possessions during the great Revolution—but re-established by Napoleon; Britain imitated that precedent in 1834, which affected principally the colonies in the West Indies.

An Adventure in Cooperation

If the acid test of peace settlements is their contribution of tranquillity for a considerable period, the post-

Napoleonic arrangements came off very well. In spite of several grave international confrontations, no clash of arms involving more than one of the great powers occurred before 1853, when the "Crimean" conflict started. Midway in the Napoleonic saga, France, the great troublemaker of the age, had passed the peak of its military strength; that and the avoidance of harsh treatment for France in the peace settlement had something to do with the peaceful atmosphere of the decades after Napoleon. So did a temporary mood of collaboration among the weight-carrying European chancelleries.

To defend the treaties of Paris and Vienna and hopefully to keep the peace in the future, the statesmen of 1814–1815 entered into two commitments for continuing cooperation. Concurrently with the making of the second Treaty of Paris, a Quadruple Alliance of the victor nations was organized. It prescribed that representatives of the four main foes of Bonaparte should meet periodically to consider their mutual interests and "measures . . . for the repose and prosperity of the nations and for the maintenance of European peace." The idea originated apparently in Britain, was avidly seized upon by Metternich, and applied especially by him in the years that followed.

Out of the vague religious mysticism of the Russian tsar emerged a second project—the quaint international compact of the Holy Alliance. This visionary and highly informal league of powers, which is often confused with the realistic Quadruple Alliance, obligated the signatories to frame their diplomatic policies in harmony with the ethical precepts of Christianity. Precisely how this pledge should be implemented, no one was prepared to explain in detail. Seasoned statesmen ridiculed the pact as "a sublime piece of mysticism and nonsense," in the description of Castlereagh. Said Metternich, "what is in fact nothing can only produce nothing," yet he and other chief ministers, though not the British, signed the curious document out of deference to the wishes of Alexander I.

Agreeable to the prescription of the Quadruple Alliance, representatives of the principal powers met in conference four times after 1818—five by one reckoning. The agenda of the meetings covered the return of France to full stature in the community of nations, and ways of grappling with revolutionary risings in each of the three peninsulas of southern Europe and in the colonial properties of Spain and Portugal in the Western Hemisphere. Step by step the British ministry diverged from the interventionist philosophy espoused by Continental cabinets, until Britain ceased to share at all in "congress" talks; that deviation brought the adventure in concerted international cooperation tumbling into ruins.

At a miniature—in terms of the political personnages attending—edition of the Vienna sessions held in September 1818 at the German town of Aix-la-Chapelle, the French problem commanded top attention. Aware that sentiment in France chafed under the presence of occupation troops and that the foreign soldiers were being infected with French revolutionary ideas, the Allied governments agreed on total evacuation. Arrangements were made with the help of a British banking house to cover the unpaid portion of the French war reparations. As a climax, France was restored to diplomatic equality with the other leading countries by being admitted to the coalition for peace, appropriately rechristened the Quintuple Alliance. The Russians sought agreement for an international commitment to beat down revolutionary forces in Spanish America; Britain and Metternich, however, stood together in rebuffing the Russian plans. It was already obvious that the several allies were laying different interpretations upon the scope of the alliance.

When revolution exploded in Spain itself in 1820, (page 31) forcing the benighted King Ferdinand to publish a progressive constitution, the St. Petersburg cabinet returned to the demand for international action against political change brought about by revolutionaries. Britain stuck by its non-intervention guns. Meddling in the domestic affairs of any country, Castlereagh proclaimed, was not the proper business of the Quintuple Alliance and no part of British intentions in diplomacy. Thus was enunciated a guideline for British foreign affairs that held throughout the nineteenth century. This cardinal policy was based upon the twin conviction that constitutional government was the best guarantee of political stability and that free countries offered greater opportunities for British traders. Following initial alarm lest the Spanish disease should prove damaging in other sections of Europe, Metternich calmed down and spoke against intervention in distant Spain as a matter of principle.

Risings in the Italian kingdom of the Two Sicilies (page 38) persuaded the Austrian prince, however, to combine with Alexander in a fresh conference at the somnolent and isolated Silesian community of Troppau (Opava in Czechoslovakia). Said the Austrian foreign minister concerning the victory of constitutionalism in the Two Sicilies, it is "the work of a subversive sect. . . . The first duty and the first interest of foreign powers is to smother it in its cradle." Of success he was sure, "owing to our firm purpose to guard the old institutions against the assault of innovators and sectarians." Unless Austria in the guise of a policeman upheld order and the status quo in disturbed Italy, revolutionary flames might leap over the low wall into the Hapsburg dominions themselves.

Only unofficial observers represented London and Paris at the Troppau meeting; Castlereagh was conspicuously absent. It was here that the three eastern monarchies laid down principles of intervention against revolutionary forces that led to their designation as the eastern bloc or the Triple Alliance of Conservatism (or more confusingly the Neo-Holy Alliance). Any government, it was announced, changed by revolution and threatening to other states would have to offer "guarantees for legal order and stability." The powers pledged themselves to bring "the guilty state back into the bosom" of the European community, peacefully if possible, by arms if necessary.

Without wholly breaking away from the Quintuple combination, Britain reiterated sharply its condemnation of intervention, which would make the great powers "the armed guardians of all thrones." The Troppau conference adjourned to permit King Ferdinand I of the Two Sicilies to confer with the eastern statesmen in order to "reconcile the interest and welfare of his subjects with the duties of the allied sovereigns toward their states and the world." In January 1821, diplomatists of the three eastern monarchies, together with the dignified Neapolitan patriarch Ferdinand I, reassembled in the charming Slovene community of Laibach (Ljubljana, Yugoslavia today). Since Italian revolutionists were imprisoned near there, tight security precautions were taken to protect the visiting celebrities. The Laibach gathering witnessed a revival of not a little of the social festivity of the Vienna Congress—parades, operas, sleighing parties.

On the recommendation of Metternich, who argued that revolutionary ferment in Italy imperiled European peace, Austria was empowered by the diplomatic bigwigs to put down insurgencies in troubled areas; Hapsburg whitecoats marched upon the Two Sicilies and Piedmont, where a revolt (page 38) had broken out, and without much difficulty overpowered the rebels. Mercurial Neapolitans welcomed King Ferdinand back to the throne with frenetic enthusiasm. Costs of the Austrian occupation forces, which hung around for five years, were borne by the local government, assisted by Rothschild bankers.

The Austrian emperor set his stamp of approval upon Metternich and his policies by naming him in 1821 state chancellor, a dignity that had been vacant since the resignation of the great Prince Kaunitz in 1792.

The final full-dress gathering of the post-Napoleonic

adventure in a European concert of powers met in 1822 at Verona, in the Austrian captive province of Venetia. Under discussion were a revolt of the Greeks against their Ottoman masters (pages 47–50), and fresh outbreaks in Spanish-America and in European Spain. Russia failed to enlist backing for proposals to aid the patriotic Greeks; it was commonly feared that an independent Greece would be indistinguishable from a client state of the empire of the tsars. Over heated protestations by the agent of George Canning, who had replaced Castlereagh at the Foreign Office, the Congress empowered Bourbon France to dispatch soldiers into Spain—a Russian offer to march Cossacks across Europe and turn them loose in Spain being rejected with scant ceremony—to smack down revolutionary elements and to restore the autocratic rule of stupid King Ferdinand VII.

These things were done, a French army of nearly 100,000 pouring into the peninsula as though on promenade; many opponents of absolutist Ferdinand were unceremoniously put to death. By this intervention, the prestige of the French Bourbon regime advanced a notch or two in European high politics. But the gulf between Britain and her Continental allies widened to unbridgeable dimensions. Canning welcomed the rift, for it seemed to him that European diplomacy had resumed a healthy condition; the doctrine of "every nation for itself and God for us all" had once more gained acceptance.

What little life remained in the Alliance ebbed away in an exchange of views in 1825 at St. Petersburg. Austria uncompromisingly opposed the sending of a tsarist force into the Ottoman realm. On policy concerning the Iberian peninsula to a limited extent, and far more so on the Italian peninsula, Metternich and Alexander could work in unison—and in fact did—to dam up revolutionary streams; but the Balkan peninsula was something different, for there vital Austrian interests, or those assumed to be vital, clashed head on with Russian purposes, and Metternich reasoned that a tsarist military struggle with the sultan would incite rebelliously minded elements all across Europe to revolt.

So the European "experiment in international government," as the episode is sometimes grandiloquently styled, passed into limbo. Against the will and wish of Britain—and to a lesser degree of France—policymakers in the three eastern monarchies pursued interventionist policies which caused the Alliance to run aground. Yet the eastern bloc preserved a measure of unity, with the voice of Russia increasingly decisive in discussions and decisions. As international collaboration sagged and then disintegrated, the positions adopted by partisans of the status quo and partisans of change took on greater solidity.

The Birth of the Monroe Doctrine

Explaining to the House of Commons why Britain had kept hands off when the French army thrust into Spain, Canning said, "I sought materials for compensation in another hemisphere. . . . I resolved that if France had Spain, it should not be Spain with the Indies. I called the New World into existence to redress the balance of the Old." It was an eloquent peroration, and contained moments of truth.

While the Napoleonic warfare raged, Latin-American insurgents had rebelled against their Spanish and Portuguese masters and had set up governments by military elites, however much the paper constitutions resembled the Constitution of the United States. The possibility that the eastern bloc might invoke force to restore Spanish authority touched off a remarkable demonstration of national spirit in the young United States. Having purchased Florida from Spain in 1819 for a trifling sum, and having extended recognition of independence to five of the former Spanish colonies, policymakers in Washington, egged on by London, resolved upon an even more striking step—or series of them.

This action took the form of the celebrated Monroe Doctrine of 1823. One passage, inspired directly by Russian trading operations in the San Francisco area, stated that the Western Hemisphere should not be the object of "future colonization by any European powers." A second point clearly affirmed that the policy of the United States with regard to Europe was "not to interfere in the internal concerns of any of its powers." This portion of the doctrine eventually fell out of favor. Finally, the Monroe pronouncement denied to European powers the right to extend their political system to any portion of the New World, under threat of war with the United States. For Metternich, the Monroe principles were more unprovoked and fully as audacious as the revolt for American independence; and other Continental statesmen echoed that evaluation. Into the twentieth century the United States has made it pellucidly clear that it intends to enforce the vital third facet of the celebrated doctrine.

A New World had come into existence as a balance against the Old, though the Monroe Doctrine had little significance immediately after it appeared. It would grow, expand, and be interpreted to meet the requirements, or the assumed needs, of the ever more powerful Yankee giant. Ever since its issuance the 1823 Doctrine has occupied a paramount place in American thinking on world diplomacy and for world diplomatists thinking about the New World.

Summary

After the fierce buffetings of the French Revolution and Napoleon, European policymakers, the Austrian Prince Metternich in the van, worked assiduously to achieve a constructive and durable peace. Under the settlements of 1814–1815, a power balance was effected so that no one country was strong enough to be able to imitate the French predominance of the preceding age. It was fully appreciated that the relationships of countries rested decisively upon the factor of military power. Though Bourbon France was surrounded by a *cordon sanitaire* and by a firm alliance of the four victorious great powers, she received comparatively mild punishment, even after the dramatic eruption of the Hundred Days. French recovery proceeded at an impressive pace, and in 1818 she was admitted to parity with the other leading powers.

Now at the zenith of his diplomatic career, Metternich tried hard through an alliance network to preserve the settlements of 1814–1815 and thereby to bolster up the position and prestige of his adopted Austria. In pursuit of those objectives Metternich relied confidently upon considerable support in pacific and conservative circles of Europe, which regarded the post-Napoleonic arrangements as sacrosanct. The possibility that the monarchical eastern bloc might apply force to recover the rebellious Spanish colonies for their king, mainly inspired the United States' formulation of the historic Monroe Doctrine.

For all their outward strength, the champions of conservatism could not indefinitely restrain the novelties that had been diffused by the French Revolution. Spoken of as liberalism, these forces fostered national sentiments and the concept of the nation-state, encouraged pressure primarily from the self-confident middle classes for constitutions, for representative political institutions, and for standard civil freedoms. The obverse of the medal was organized resistance to change by arbitrary, authoritarian governments directed by Metternich and like-minded makers of public decisions in central and eastern Europe. If a political map of Europe after the Second World War is compared with one of 1815, it will be seen that nearly all the changes occurred in the central and eastern sections of the Continent.

C H A P T E R . . . 2

Convalescence and Convulsions

The French Restoration

A German philosopher once described the Napoleonic era as the sixth day of Creation, for a man had arisen; it was followed by the Sabbath day of calm when all creative power seemed at rest. The German was guilty of a half-truth, for in France, following the storm and stress of Bonaparte's rule, the nation groped its way back to stability, though not without eruptions.

Returning to Paris in the baggage of the Allies for a second time, Louis XVIII was well received, for he seemed to imply peace, so welcome after a generation of turmoil in which nearly every French family had lost at least one male member. Down to 1870 France would be ruled, except for a few months, by four former émigrés, and of them only Louis XVIII died with the crown on his head. Firm believer as he was in the "divine right" philosophy of government, Louis XVIII unhesitatingly hoisted the white flag of the old regime in place of the revolutionary tri-color. Yet, as an exile in England, he had come to understand that a king must reconcile himself to the changed conditions in France and must strive to make himself respected, or at least tolerated, by all classes. Prudent he was—and lazy.

The crown could rely upon the French aristocracy, led by the heir-presumptive to the throne, the Comte d'Artois, and the support of the churchmen. Newly appointed bishops were mostly nobles and royalists. The traditional alignment of crown and altar was quickly reknit. According to the Napoleonic Concordat (renewed in 1819), the clergy depended upon the government for their incomes and maintenance of church buildings; pressure was exerted to recover the pre-Revolutionary landed properties of the church. Many a middle-class Frenchman resented the zealous activity of the returned Jesuits; in fact, "Jesuit" became the anti-clerical epithet for anything about the church that provoked displeasure.

Foes of the Restoration regime came from Bonapartists, who were particularly numerous among former army officers; republicans; and unenfranchised bourgeoisie, who felt that they should have influence in state affairs commensurate with their wealth and talents. As matters stood, the electorate was under 100,000 —a much broader suffrage, nonetheless, than in England—but it excluded most middle-class men as well as urban workers and peasants from voting.

To a degree, the two houses of the French royal parliament resembled the Lords and Commons of Britain. After the first election, unregenerate, vengeful aristocrats dominated the national legislature. For many a returned noble the constitution itself was anathema, since it was grounded on "the atheistic dogma" of popular sovereignty. The Bourbon regime struck hard against Bonapartists during months of "White Terror." The most eminent martyr of the passion for revenge was popular Marshal Ney, who was charged with high treason in an exciting, dramatic trial under the aegis of the aristocratic Chamber of Peers. Courageously the rough, bold soldier, who had faced death a hundred times, defended himself, but he was condemned and executed by a firing squad in Paris.

That episode widened the gulf between the two Frances—the old Bourbon regime, and the new France born of the Revolution and Napoleon. Army reorganization, featuring the dissolution of the Bonapartist forces and adoption of a new military system, heightened aversion to the Restoration; for personal security the king created a new Royal Guard.

It was a feather in the royal cap to secure the early evacuation of the foreign conquerors of Napoleon. Altogether about 150,000 troops were garrisoned in France; the Austrian whitecoats were especially detested because of their propensity for looting. Occupying forces were reduced in 1817, and the following year, after the French government arranged to finance the balance of the war indemnity, all foreign soldiers were withdrawn, two years ahead of the original schedule. At the same time, France was recognized as an equal partner with the other great powers in the high counsels of Europe. The quick repression of revolutionaries in Spain by French soldiers in 1823 also lifted Bourbon prestige a trifle.

The resilience of France after defeats in great wars is, or ought to be, a matter of proverb. Napoleon, to be sure, had strengthened the economy by eradicating the lingering vestiges of serfdom, and by promoting technical education, industrial exhibitions, and so forth. But right after Waterloo, industry was dislocated as orders for war supplies slacked off; unemployment became widespread and hardships were intensified by a short harvest in 1816–1817. Yet within five years after fighting ceased, an air of prosperity enveloped France, thanks primarily to her tough hard-working peasants. State finances were put on a sound footing, industry experienced a moderate yet steady growth, and many new canals were dug, though roadways were generally neglected. Then as now, Paris was the headquarters of banking and commerce. Since capital was scarce and known resources of coal and iron ore small, French industrial development was retarded. Manufacturers preferred to turn out luxury articles instead of goods by mass production; protective tariffs kept down foreign competition and tended to numb managerial initiative.

When Louis XVIII died in 1824, France was an orderly, prosperous country; domestic calamities had been avoided. The elderly, corpulent Bourbon had not done too badly in filling the spacious shoes of the dynamic little Corsican. Among intellectuals and army men, however, radical secret societies spread, partly in reaction to the ultra-royalist temper of parliament; in 1821 rioting broke loose, but was soon repressed and its leaders imprisoned.

Troubles in the Iberian Peninsula

Spaniards, on the whole, displayed the intense pride of a nation that had battled heroically against the legions of Napoleon, and they gloried in a history that had set its stamp upon half the world from Holland by way of South America to the Philippines. Yet Spain was in decline and edged from disaster to disaster. King Ferdinand VII, reinstated on the throne in 1814, belonged to the branch of the Bourbon family that stubbornly declined to come to terms with new currents, regardless of the mythical image of "liberalism" he had built up in exile. The Spanish liberal fringe accepted him as monarch without conspicuous grace and only because no plausible alternative appeared on the horizon. So different from his predecessor, Joseph Bonaparte, as ruler of Spain Ferdinand VII followed anachronistic, impulsive, and repressive policies.

In the thinking of the king, absolutism in politics and religion was indispensable for stability in a country noted for rampant individualism. Wherefore the progressive constitution of 1812, regarded as an ideal document by many rebellious spirits all across Europe, was swept away, and the authority of the church and the Jesuits was reconstituted. Incompetent administration aggravated evils in a country that was economically stagnant and very heavily illiterate. Public finances were mismanaged and revenues dwindled with the revolt of Spain's vast colonial holdings in the New World.

Visionary royal plans to recover the colonies precipitated in 1820 a military insurrection, which ushered in recurrent political upheavals that lasted for two generations. Already army morale was low due to bad pay, bad training, bad housing; troops tapped for service across the Atlantic openly rebelled. Sympathetic risings in Madrid and in northern cities demanded the resurrection of the constitution of 1812, to which king and counsellors straightaway assented. This instrument of government allotted only slight authority to the crown and prescribed a parliament (*Cortes*) elected on a fairly broad franchise, liberty of press, and equality of citizens. At the insistence of the rebel leadership, the hated court of the Inquisition was suppressed and partial confiscation of ecclesiastical estates was promised. But the Spanish colonies on the American continent were lost forever.

The successful revolt in Spain alarmed the eastern bloc of powers, as has been indicated (page 20). With its blessing, soldiers of France marched beyond the Pyrenees and easily overpowered the bickering champions of a liberal society. Jubilantly, Ferdinand VII canceled progressive reforms and exiled or ruthlessly executed thousands who had dared to challenge royal tyranny. In harmony with the divine right philosophy, he defied (or so it seems) Spanish public law by designating his infant daughter, Isabella II, as the next sovereign.

But his brother Don Carlos, an authoritarian and clerical, claiming (1833) that he was the rightful successor to the throne, plunged Spain into bitter civil war. Each side sought and won supporters until nearly

all articulate Spaniards were drawn into the implacable
vendetta, known as the first Carlist war. Deep down
there was more to the savage conflict than controversy
over who should wear the crown. Around the antiliberal
Carlos gathered comfortably fixed peasants and clerical
standpatters who resented the changes that the forces of
liberalism in the expanding towns stood for. Part of the
time, sections of the interesting Basque minority, which
resented liberal devotion to centralization of government, aided and abetted the Carlist cause. To rally
support for the queen, liberally-inclined ministers restored (1837) the constitution of 1812 in a somewhat
watered-down version.

Foreign powers kept hands off the Spanish civil war
and in 1839 the insurgents acknowledged defeat. Yet
the flame of anti-liberalism flickered on to burst forth
in the seventies in a second spasm of Carlism. In the
meantime, Isabella II was implicated in a tug-of-war
between Paris and London. While the French cabinet
eagerly desired (1846) her to marry a French prince, the
British loudly said no. The dispute envenomed Anglo-
French politics and played a part in the downfall of
King Louis Philippe (page 97).

Troubles in Spain had reverberations in adjoining
Portugal, whose sovereign had fled to his colony of
Brazil during the era of Napoleon. An army revolt of
1820 called upon the dynasty to return to Europe and
resulted in the publication of a constitution copied in
1822 from the Spanish original. Going back to Lisbon,
King John VI swore to obey and to enforce the constitution, though he never intended in fact to do so.
Counter-revolutionaries made life perilous for the monarch. Brazilian patriots seized the opportunity to de-
clare in 1822 the independence of their vast land, and
they chose a son of John VI as their constitutional
emperor; the lordship of Iberia from the Rio Grande
to Tierra del Fuego had ceased to exist.

Back in Portugal, a fresh constitution of 1826 embodied less popular rule than its predecessor, but even

that antagonized partisans of despotism and clerical ascendancy. Civil warfare presently descended upon the country and bedeviled its existence for years; yet, a constitution remained in operation and its friends hit their ecclesiastical opponents by banishing the Jesuits again and transferring church estates to the government. No more than Spain was Portugal a persuasive advertisement of the virtues of parliamentary government and a "liberal" constitution.

Ferment in Italy

In the course of the era of the French Revolution and Napoleon, a few Italians were aroused from the political torpor that had gripped their ancestors for generations. French ideas fertilized a sentiment as old as Alighieri Dante, noblest of Italian poets and prophets, that the peninsula should emancipate itself from foreign barbarians and become master of its own destiny. And Napoleon, a man of Italian origins, had subjected virtually all of the peninsula to his sharp sword, thus fostering the vision of political consolidation.

For the foundations of a unified Italy, spokesmen for independence pointed to the common language (divisive dialects apart), a common religious faith, and a cultural heritage transcending in richness that of any other nationality in the western world. Nevertheless, at the dawn of the nineteenth century, Italy meant merely several disparate parcels of real estate, politically impotent, and not very inspiring in the realms of literature and the arts. So far as ordinary fellows were concerned, political allegiance was owed to town or region, not to the Italian nation.

Slowly, yet inexorably, a spirit of *risorgimento*—of resurgence—penetrated an enlightened elite, aware of French and British ways, and combated inertia, political apathy, and indolence. Whereas noble Italian landowners and their clerical allies dominated the post-Waterloo generation, the wave of the future belonged to the bourgeoisie—men of the professional classes, physicians, lawyers especially, high-minded authors and composers, ex-army officers and civil servants, members of the business community favorably disposed to change, and articulate students who had less to lose by a far-ranging transformation than their elders.

A country of 18,000,000, Italy had been divided by the Vienna settlement into eight states with divergencies in government, in laws and administration, and in economy. Tariff policies gravely hampered commercial expansion; goods moving 150 miles from Florence to Milan passed through eight customs offices! Since tariffs tended to run high, smuggling flourished. Credit was scarce, though here as elsewhere the ubiquitous Rothschild family was prepared to make well-secured loans at attractive rates of interest.

Austria and its Hapsburg dynasty exercised a powerful voice in Italian public life. Lombardy-Venetia in the north constituted a kingdom directly subject to the cabinet in Vienna. If Austrian rule was less effective and less enlightened than in the Lombardy of the eighteenth century, it did permit a measure of freedom, was comparatively honest, and abolished the more glaring privileges of aristocrats and churchmen. In this region, once famed for excellence in small-scale industry, mechanization of production proceeded very slowly. Much grain continued to be ground, for example, on river barges that were moved from place to place as need required. Few steam engines were imported, yet silk manufacturing and agriculture prospered in the Po Valley, a web of canals was laid out, and an assertive middle class emerged in Milan, Venice, and other urban communities.

No doubt the grand duchy of Tuscany, ruled by an Austrian Hapsburg, was the most progressive and efficient state in the entire peninsula. Its citizens enjoyed an unmatched degree of toleration in regard to the press and religion, and benefited from exemplary legal and prison systems. Tuscany possessed, too, the best

Italian universities and prided itself on its advanced culture, centering upon the capital, glorious Florence. Under public auspices, a vast project to drain swamp-land was carried out, and Livorno (Leghorn) grew as a trading and shipbuilding community.

It can scarcely be doubted that temporal authority over the broad States of the Church weakened in the long run the prestige of the Papacy—and not only in Italy. For a time the most influential personality in the Papal States was Cardinal Ercole Consalvi (1757–1824), who as Secretary of State ranked second only to the pope in the Vatican hierarchy. So brilliantly had the Cardinal championed papal interests at the Congress of Vienna that the austere Castlereagh declared, "He was the master of us all." It was no light task to improve human conditions in the Papal States; in ancient Rome, for instance, it was reliably estimated that one out of three of the population depended for his daily bread upon charity or thievery. Yet Consalvi shouldered the work of improvement in good heart.

Under the leadership of the Cardinal, Rome was scrubbed up and better policed, and Vatican finances were put in order. He wished not only to make administration more effective, but to remove it from the hands of the clergy, and, therewith, to curtail clerical power in the judicial functions of government. He even ventured to propose that bodies of laymen should be organized in provinces and cities to advise on public policies, but nothing came of that recommendation. Enough had been accomplished, however, to keep the States of the Church quiet when political volcanoes erupted elsewhere in Italy.

True to his intellectual type, Consalvi stubbornly opposed press freedom as a pernicious instrument for adversaries of Roman Catholicism and of papal temporal rule. Newspapers in Rome and Bologna, consequently, kept mum on political questions. Out of middle-class circles issued protests against ecclesiastical censorship and demands for a share in governmental affairs. From Vienna Prince Metternich repeatedly urged the Vatican to lead the way in some form of a *Lega Italica* for purposes of security against external and domestic enemies, but the appeals fell flat.

By reason of their secular responsibilities, popes and their aides could not concentrate on the spiritual duties of an immense religious fellowship, and those secular obligations also affected Vatican attitudes on Italian national unity and European politics generally, in ways that proved injurious for papal claims to impartiality in international issues. Besides, maladministration of secular affairs or unfairness in the treatment of citizens in the States of the Church was bound to be seized upon by anticlerical adversaries of the Vatican everywhere and exploited for all or more than it was worth.

The largest and most populous of the Italian states, the kingdom of the Two Sicilies, was probably the worst governed of the lot. Even the mildest of reformers were tagged as conspiratorial incendiaries, as "Jacobins," which connoted about the same as "Bolsheviks" in the twentieth century. Although the Two Sicilies was the most urbanized section of Italy, Naples ranking probably fourth among European cities, five out of six families wrested a subsistence living from the soil. Many worked as laborers on big, heavily mortgaged proprietorships. Wooden plows and hand flails were common tools, and every few years the principal crops—grain and grapes—fell way below normal yields.

Squalor, scarcity of water, malaria, pellagra, and earthquakes were constant companions of the inhabitants of the Two Sicilies. Black bread made of barley was the staple food, and inability to read and write was well-nigh universal. Propertyless citizens of Naples called *lazzaroni* (ragged beggars) had established a reputation for excitability, happy-go-lucky habits, and willingness to demonstrate lustily in any political cause regardless of its objectives.

Over the protestations of its aristocratic and educated classes, the island of Sicily had been politically merged with the adjacent mainland, though it had a separate administration. Sicilian orators loudly declared that their homeland was governed as a conquered province.

The great hope for Italian national unity was the small northwestern kingdom of Piedmont (Sardinia) with its capital at Turin. Abutting on France, this region had lived under French rule for a generation; all the outstanding Piedmontese in the eventual work of national consolidation were born under the French flag, and a substantial part of the population spoke French by preference. Piedmont was less subject to control by Austria than any of her sister states. The ruling classes of landed aristocracy and clerics were already being challenged, albeit moderately, by an emerging, nationalistically oriented bourgeoisie.

Wherever in Europe neither a parliamentary regime nor freedom of publication prevailed, secret societies were preferred institutions to prepare the way for change. In Italy, besides, conspiracy was the most valid channel for patriotic expression. Of the several subterranean societies that burgeoned up on Italian soil, the largest and historically the most important was the *Carbonari* (charcoal-burners), which by 1815 had lodges all over the peninsula and several hundred thousand members drawn from the middle classes, an occasional priest, highbrow aristocrats, low-brow brigands, and professional conspirators. Publications of the organization were printed in Milan and distributed among the unco-ordinated groups.

At *Carbonari* meetings, there was much romantic, mystical rigmarole and elaborate ritual, savoring of a juvenile society. Members saluted one another as "Good Cousins." Above all else, the *Carbonari* were dedicated to a unified and independent Italy. They opposed despotism and wanted popular sovereignty; they opposed authoritarianism and wanted the liberties of 1789; they opposed clerical political power and wanted curbs clamped upon churchmen.

Risings in 1820–1821

More or less inspired by the surprisingly successful 1820 military mutiny in Spain, Neapolitan *Carbonari* rebelled against the Bourbon regime of elderly King Ferdinand I. An extremely religious man, he had embittered some of his politically alert subjects by negotiating a concordat with the Vatican recognizing Catholicism as the exclusive religion, handing over control of education and censorship to ecclesiastics, and hinting at the restoration of expropriated church property. On the other hand, the government was comparatively mild; police were not too tough on men who spoke in derogatory language of the existing pattern of society.

On a visit to Naples in 1819, Metternich learned with alarm about secret conspiratorial societies. They struck the following year. The royal army melted away, but the insurgents attracted almost no cooperation from the underfed, unwashed Neapolitan multitude. King Ferdinand grudgingly yielded to an imperious demand for a Spanish-type constitution. That gain encouraged brashness in the press, sensationalism in place of thought, and, when a parliament was convened, deputies were showered with flamboyant rhetoric and much meaningless academic debate. Voices of Sicily pleaded for a fully separate government, while hapless peasants indulged in destructive anarchy.

Under these circumstances, the eastern power bloc, as has been indicated (page 22), commissioned Austria to send troops into the Two Sicilies to put an end to turbulence. When the Hapsburg forces approached Naples, the parliamentary army put up only token resistance. Some *Carbonari* leaders ran away; others were apprehended and so inhumanly abused by local authorities that Austrian officials intervened to temper punishments. Whitecoats of Austria remained in the Two Sicilies until 1826.

Another revolt, quite unco-ordinated with the Neapolitan affair, had broken loose meantime in Piedmont. Disorderly students in Turin started the open revolutionary commotion. *Carbonari* "cousins" took charge, certain unrealistic extremists demanding that Austria should be at once expelled from the peninsula bag and baggage. The sequel closely paralleled the experience in the Two Sicilies.

In the city of Milan, vigilant Austrian police uncovered a *Carbonari* plot to overthrow Hapsburg authority; the leaders were seized and sentenced to long prison terms. Among the *Carbonari* who fled to Britain was Anthony Panizzi (1797–1879), who moved up to the post of principal librarian of the British Museum in London; his grand conception of the Museum reading room contributed greatly to making that institution a veritable paradise for scholars. Seemingly, though no more than that, the Italian forces of repression appeared to have conquered the partisans of constitutionalism and a united Italy.

The Evolution of Germany

In divided Germany, as in divided Italy, the convalescence of conservatism far outstripped in importance any manifestations of the revolutionary spirit. The latter cropped up, true enough, but outbreaks were relatively small daubs, easily exaggerated, on the large picture.

Taking Germany as a whole, the middle classes were more numerous in the urbanized Rhineland than elsewhere, except of course, in capital cities such as Bavarian Munich and Saxon Dresden. Growth of the middle classes was retarded by the disruption of domestic and foreign trade and paralysis in manufacturing that accompanied the Napoleonic warfare and by periodic recessions in business, due partly to British competition. Hard times induced thousands of families in western Germany to seek new opportunities in the United

States, a harbinger of the vastly larger emigration to the New World that began in the 1840's.

As in other parts of Europe, it was the bourgeoisie principally that set up clamor for constitutions, for popular sovereignty, for national unity, and for government policies that would encourage the expansion of capitalistic economy. German states in geographical proximity to France—Baden, Württemberg, and Bavaria—obtained constitutions which accorded limited legislative powers to elected bodies, but preserved effective authority in the crown and royal ministries. A rather enlightened despotism prevailed in Bavaria, whose kings sponsored exciting programs for the beautification of their capital, Munich (page 133). More than once, the Prussian king promised to issue a constitution, but the pledge was not implemented; instead provincial diets of an advisory character, chosen by the landed aristocracy and well-to-do peasants, continued to meet. It was not until 1847 that a central united Prussian diet was convened for the first time.

Allied to the crown in the management of the kingdom of Prussia was the Junker land-owning nobility, which largely supplied officers for the royal army and top administrative officers. Sons of burghers filled state posts in the lower echelons and shared in decision making on municipal affairs. The skillful and efficient bureaucracy of Prussia set standards that other German states sought to imitate. The peasant masses in overwhelmingly rural "Germany" seemed content to allow public business to be conducted by their social betters. Speaking broadly, small peasant farms predominated in the Rhineland and in the southern states, middle-sized holdings to the west of the Elbe River, and large Junker proprietorships in the north reaching away to the province of East Prussia.

Perhaps more sharply than in other sections of the Continent, it was the comfortably-fixed, educated classes that responded to and promoted the German national awakening. Should not the proud achievements of their co-nationals in philosophy and science, they asked, be matched by strong, unified political institutions? That national attitude contrasted with the traditional cosmopolitanism of German men of learning, best personified by the versatile Johann W. Goethe. Higher education bounded forward with the foundation of new universities at Berlin, destined to develop into the most respected institution of learning in the world, and at Bonn in the Rhineland, and at Munich. As never before, German university professors stressed original investigations, disseminated their findings in lecture halls and in writings, directed seminars in which to train young scholars, and pursued learning and truth for their own sake. They prized ideals of professorial freedom and of intellectual liberty for their students.

As another meaningful facet of the German educational revival, first-rate technological institutes were organized at Dresden and Karlsruhe in particular. German institutions of university grade served as models for the rest of Europe and after the mid-century for overseas countries from the United States to Japan. Secondary and primary schooling, notably of Prussia, attracted investigation by educational experts from many foreign countries.

In the post-Waterloo era, many a German student displayed romantic enthusiasm for national unification. Certain of their elders fostered the intensification of national sentiments, Friedrich L. Jahn (1778–1852) for one. A Prussian patriot in his youth, Jahn turned into an ardent German nationalist while his country lay helpless under the Napoleonic jackboot. To build up physically robust nationalists, he established gymnastic societies (*Turnverein*), which spread extensively; they evolved into political and cultural organizations as well. In his writings, Vater Jahn glorified the history and language of Germany, its customs and cultural distinctiveness. Decked out in the costume of the early Germans, with staff in hand, his gymnasts walked from place to place proclaiming the German national ideal.

Jahn had an industrious spiritual ally in the Rhine-
lander Professor Ernst M. Arndt (1769–1860), whose
national consciousness had likewise been quickened by
the humiliations inflicted by Bonaparte. In warmly
patriotic verse, he preached that wherever the German
language was spoken there was the German fatherland
(*Was ist des deutschen Vaterland?*). For inflammatory
diatribes, Arndt was dismissed from the faculty of Bonn
University, but he had already exerted a profound influence upon a novel institution, the *Burschenschaften*.

An organization of university students, the *Burschenschaften* was founded at Jena shortly before Waterloo.
Bursche, meaning lad, was the familiar term used for a
German academic youth. This movement, which possessed little coherence, was intended not only to perpetuate the patriotic spirit that gripped Germans in
the war of liberation against Napoleon, but also to
diffuse the creed of a united Germany and popular
participation in affairs of state. As a badge of distinction members wore their hair long; they pledged themselves to live as Christians and German patriots.

For some of them, the concept of "Germany" embraced Austrian and Swiss areas of German speech—
grossdeutsch is the word for it—and even the Dutch
and the Flemings of Belgium! On the banner of the
fraternity, which established chapters in sixteen universities, were inscribed the watchwords, "Honor,
Liberty, Fatherland." The colors of the *Burschenschaften*—black and red, with gold trimmings—would
one day be adopted for the flag of the German revolutionary upheaval in 1848, of the Weimar Republic after
the First World War, and of the Federal or West German Republic following the Second World War.

In the autumn of 1817, some five hundred *Burschen*
staged a colorful demonstration at the Wartburg in
Eisenach to commemorate at once the victory over
Napoleon at Leipzig four years before and the tercen-
tenary of the posting of Luther's famous theses at Wit-
tenberg—popularly regarded as the first episode in the

Reformation. Hymn singing and prayers to the God of Luther blended with intoxicating patriotic addresses and beer drinking. Recalling how Luther had audaciously tossed a papal bull to the flames, students threw unpopular books, a corporal's baton, and other hated symbols of the established order into a bonfire. Echoing the opinion of his master, Metternich, Friedrich Gentz ascribed this student outburst to "false wisdom" taught by "wicked professors." Like Socrates of old time, men of learning were charged with polluting the minds of youth with dangerous thoughts.

Before the alarm aroused in official circles by the Wartburg festival had died away, a theological student at Jena, Karl Sand, who belonged to the *Burschen,* assassinated in 1819 a mediocre German playwright and poet, Auguste F. F. Kotzebue. As an agent of the Russian tsar, Kotzebue had been sending reports to St. Petersburg denouncing the patriotic student agitation. German princes and their old-fashioned advisers saw red. An attempt upon the life of a reactionary minister of the little Nassau state seemed to confirm the official judgment that a widespread conspiracy against authority was in the making.

Metternich decided that the time had come to strike hard at subversive activities. "By the help of God," he declared grandiloquently, "I hope to defeat the German revolution, even as I have vanquished the conqueror of the world." Summoning representatives of the Federal Diet to a meeting at Carlsbad in Bohemia in 1819, he laid before them a series of laws, which have gone down in history as the Carlsbad Decrees. These measures placed universities under strict surveillance, with inspectors to watch over the lectures of professors and utterances of students; dissolved the *Burschenschaften* and gymnastic societies; and set up a rigid censorship on newspapers and pamphlets. To ferret out conspiracies, which the Austrian prince professed to believe permeated German Europe, a central investigating committee was set up at Mainz in the Rhineland.

After the Federal Diet formally approved these obnoxious decrees, public authorities relentlessly persecuted anything interpreted as dangerous for the established order. Prized traditions of university freedom vanished, and many a student and other liberal abandoned active interest in politics. For a full generation, this legislation, which gratified the spirit of Metternich and like-minded conservatives, remained on the statute books. Yet in the revolutionary storms of 1848, many men who had affiliated with patriotic societies in their student days manned barricades. Violently assailed by liberals at the time as indefensible infringements upon the natural rights of learners, the Carlsbad Decrees, thought of in perspective, seem innocuous compared with restraints upon education imposed by Fascist and Communist dictatorships of the twentieth century.

Long since, a new institution with significant implications for the future of Germany had come into existence under the aegis of Prussia. This novelty was a *Zollverein* or customs union, whose starting point was a Prussian law of 1818 which abolished internal tariffs that had hampered the expansion of trade, and created a single, low tariff for the whole kingdom. On invitation, adjacent German states, one by one, entered the *Zollverein* and removed barriers to commerce, so that by 1834 over twenty-three million Germans, living in an area larger than New York, Pennsylvania, and New England combined, were exchanging goods freely.

As by-products of the customs union, a uniform system of weights and measures was adopted and two currencies replaced the score previously in use. Manufacturing, foreign trade, and mining made notable advances; businessmen inside the *Zollverein* bloc learned to think in terms of the larger German community. Significantly, Austria was excluded from the commercial union—half because of political considerations and half because German policymakers feared competition from producers of grain, especially from the Hungarian portion of the Hapsburg Empire. More and more, partisans of the German national cause looked to Prussia, not Vienna, for leadership and guidance on the road to unity.

Turk and Serb

Pick up a European map of 1815; over the southeastern area—the Balkan Peninsula—and across into Asia Minor sprawls the term "Ottoman Empire." At that point the writ of the Turkish sultan also ran down into the Arabian Peninsula and over the northern fringe of Africa, deep into Algeria. Slightly more than a century and a quarter before, the hosts of Islam had besieged the walled Christian citadel of Vienna, but their defeat there in 1683 openly heralded the Turkish retreat from central Europe, the beginning of the decline and fall of the once-dreaded Ottoman realm.

Since Turkey was a Moslem theocracy, it was regarded as beyond the pale of European civilization; the sultan had not been invited, for instance, to sign the Treaty of the Holy Alliance. Within the Balkan portion of his empire lived nationalities of the Christian persuasion, albeit of the Orthodox Eastern branch of the faith—Greeks and Serbs, Bulgars and Rumanians principally. On the western side of the peninsula in wild and rugged country was a small nationality, the Albanians, essentially Moslem in religion and governed with a loose Turkish rein. The intelligentsia of the Orthodox nationalities—their parish priests, their middleclasses, together a small fraction of all—had awakened to national consciousness, which betokened further losses of Turkish territory and authority.

Corruption and indolence on the part of Ottoman administrators impaired the fabric of the government and so did the decadent quality of the fighting services. Important in that connection was a special army corps, the janissaries, once a powerful instrument of the sultan but long since degenerated into a contingent of arrogant plunderers and lawless rebels. Unless and until this foul brood was disciplined or dispersed and the Christian populations were accorded something approaching decent social and economic treatment, the decay of the Ottoman realm could not be arrested.

First of the Balkan peoples to gain their freedom, or more exactly semi-independence, were the little known Serbs, the hard core of the Yugoslav family. Living in a primitive society where affluence was measured by the number of hogs or sheep one owned, the ancestors of the nineteenth-century Serbs had attained political eminence and cultural brilliance late in the Middle Ages; singers of ballads and pseudo-historians embellished the illustrious past with legendary grandeur. The initial Serb rebellion of 1804 was pointed against the rapacious janissaries and only gradually turned into a popular crusade to throw off the Ottoman yoke. Directing the rebel patriots over terrain that nature designed for guerrilla fighting was a respected and bold pig-dealer, Karageorge or Black George (1760–1817), a natural leader of men. From Russian sources, assistance flowed to the gallant Slav and Orthodox brothers until the warfare with Napoleon required all tsarist resources at home. Turkish armies then smashed down the insurgency and invoked a fearsome reign of terror in the hope of preventing a repeat performance.

The event belied that expectation, for in 1815 a fresh upheaval started under the guidance of a second well-to-do swineherd, Milosh Obrenovich. Military victories together with shrewd diplomacy persuaded the Ottoman government in 1817 to concede effective home rule to a small Serb state lying just south of the Danube and including the large town of Belgrade, which served as the seat of government. Rebel chieftain Milosh assumed the dignity of hereditary prince. In 1829 these arrangements were given international endorsement. Serbia was obliged to pay tribute to the sultan, and Turkish soldiers garrisoned Belgrade until 1867.

The Serb state carved out of Turkey covered only a

fraction of the territory on which Yugoslavs dwelt. In fact, many more Yugoslavs lived under the flags of Austria and Turkey than in the little autonomous principality; acquisition of the lands occupied by kinsmen became and remained the overarching ambition of Serbian nationalists. One point more: From the struggles for independence emerged two families that competed for political supremacy in Serbia—the descendants of Karageorge and of Obrenovich. After Milosh and his son had both been forced to abdicate, Alexander Karageorge, son of Black George, assumed the princeship in 1842. Feuding between these rival dynasties disturbed Serbian politics straight into the twentieth century. Factionalism and political jobbery, finally, imposed severe handicaps on social progress, though in 1844 a university opened its doors in Belgrade.

The Winning of Greek Independence

Whereas the Serbs have contributed only modestly to world culture, the Greeks of antiquity had done famously. That record redounded to the political advantage of contemporary Greeks, who were identified in Christian countries with the ancient Athenians. Molders of opinion in these lands studied as youths the ancient Greek classics in school, college, and university, and in maturity treasured them for their literary beauty and their wisdom. From London through Paris and Moscow to Boston, affection for Greece, or philhellenism, was a potent asset for Greeks struggling to be free.

While most Greeks were overwhelmingly poor and unlettered countryfolk—many of them covetous of the land worked by neighboring Moslems—small business and intellectual classes had emerged. The former prospered materially by reason of the French revolutionary wars; the latter—or some of them—had imbibed the intoxicating French ideas of 1789.

Not all Yankees rallied to the struggle for independence from Great Britain; not all Greek-feeling folk rallied to the campaigns for freedom from Ottoman lordship. But many had been aroused to an appreciation of the ancient grandeur of their nation by thrilling folk ballads, by translations of classics into the current vernacular, or by the persuasions of parish priests, the peculiar guardians and propagators of national prides and prejudices. Their ecclesiastical superiors, owing their bishoprics to the sultan, haughtily held aloof from the secular political struggle.

As in other despotisms, secret patriotic societies of conspirators furnished the main leadership and dynamic of the Greek national cause. Of them, the most significant was *Philiké Hetairia,* a sort of Greek counterpart of the Italian *Carbonari.* Not much is known about this organization, save that it was founded about 1815 by Greek merchants congregated in the new Russian seaport of Odessa, and that it enrolled tens of thousands of adherents.

Led by men affiliated with this society, Greek rebels launched an insurrection in 1821, counting on assistance from the big Orthodox brother, Russia. When tsarist aid failed to materialize, the uprising collapsed ignominiously as it was bound to do. But a second and much more substantial rebellion erupted in Greece proper, in the Morea, in the mountainous Peloponnesus, and in Greek-peopled islands of the Aegean Sea.

Unofficial circles in Christian Europe were shocked by the execution of the Orthodox patriarch in Constantinople on order of the sultan; indignation was especially acute in the empire of the tsars. Yet, for the time being, no major government showed any disposition to help the struggling Greeks. Metternich preached a "hands-off" policy and other cabinets agreed that that course was the part of wisdom.

In 1823, however, the London ministry, with an eye to commercial interests as in its policy on the Spanish colonies in America, recognized the insurgent Greeks as belligerents. The Austrian chancellor protested energetically but vainly against this unilateral action.

Given the disparity in the resources of Greek and Turk, the successes of the spirited rebels on land and sea must be described as surprising. Guerrilla warfare characterized much of the conflict, marked by atrocious massacres committed by both belligerents. "Kill them all" seemed to be the motto of both sides in this war of extermination; "God will know his own." The military capability of the Turk was somewhat impaired by the belated dissolution in 1826 of the unruly janissaries on the heels of a mutiny.

When Greek victory appeared to be certain, the government of the sultan persuaded its vassal, the ambitious governor of Egypt, Mehemet Ali, to throw his sword into the scales. Straightaway the military panorama changed radically, the Egyptians carrying all before them and perpetrating barbarous inhumanities in the process, which stirred the conscience and hearts of Philhellenes and Christians to the depths. The death in 1824 of British Lord Byron, perhaps the favorite European man of letters, while fighting the good fight, dramatically advertised the Greek insurgency.

Pro-Greek sentiment all over Europe—and in the United States—precipitated a response of volunteers, weapons, cash, and, most important of all, pressure on cabinets to intervene in the ghastly civil war. Fearful lest the empire of the tsars would unsheath the sword against the Turks and establish a free Greece as a Russian satellite, the London ministry proposed joint action by the great powers to stop the bloodshed and create an autonomous Greek state.

Holding that a triumphant Greek rebellion would inspirit insurgents in other sections of Europe, Metternich responded negatively to the British overture, and Prussia sided with him. But Britain, France, and Russia cooperated in 1827 in despatching warcraft to the fighting zone and in arranging an armistice, which was soon ruptured. In the same year, an Allied fleet was ordered into Navarino Bay, a fine harbor on the western coast of Morea, to force a second cease-fire. Turkish-Egyptian men-of-war were stationed in the port, and apparently they opened fire on Allied naval units. Be that as it may, there ensued an extraordinary sea fight lasting four hours. Turkish seapower was destroyed in the greatest maritime defeat for the Ottoman Empire since the Battle of Lepanto two and a half centuries before. The clash virtually assured victory for the Greek cause; French troops cleansed the Morea of Turkish forces, and armies of the tsar advanced upon Turkey from the north, pressing to within easy range of Constantinople (Istanbul).

Whereupon, the sultan tossed in the sponge and agreed in the 1829 Treaty of Adrianople to the establishment of a small independent Greek kingdom. That arch champion of legitimacy and the status quo, the Austrian chancellor, was deeply wounded by this transgression of his basic philosophy, but nothing practicable could be done about it. Viewed in perspective, the Duke of Wellington, a confirmed partisan of Turkey, was not wide of the mark when he bluntly described the Adrianople settlement as "the deathblow to the independence of the Ottoman Porte, and the forerunner of the dissolution and extinction of its power."

Under the aegis of the great powers, a dynasty for Greece was imported from Bavaria in 1832. Young King Otto and his German officials governed in a frivolous and incompetent manner; it was an "idle pageant," blurted out a Briton well-informed on the Greek realities. It was not until 1843 that a constitution, allowing some popular share in government, was granted.

The war for independence cost the Greeks heavily in life and property. Methods of farming were unprogressive, though peasants who obtained land which Moslems had formerly worked had reason for satisfaction. Industry and shipping were in a lowly state, so that many a hard-pressed family sought greener pastures in the Ottoman Empire. More than that, the monarchy of 1829 contained less than a third of the Greek-speaking (and presumably Greek-feeling) population. As with the

Serbs, so Greek patriots dreamed of complete national fulfillment, which reached fruition only in 1960.

The creation of a free Greece stimulated national patriotism among politically articulate Rumanians and, less so, Bulgarians. By the 1829 Treaty of Adrianople, Turkey bestowed a larger measure of autonomy on the Rumanian-peopled Danubian principalities of Moldavia and Wallachia. Russia, who in 1812 had snatched away from the sultan the adjoining region of Bessarabia, partly inhabited by Rumanians, now sent agents into the principalities where they obtained a commanding position in public affairs. Yet Rumanian national sentiments kept rising, especially among the intellectual elite who read about western ways and manners or went off to Paris to study. It became fashionable to call the town of Bucharest the "Paris of the East," as under the Communist dispensation of the twentieth-century Bucharest would be known as the "Moscow of the South."

As for the Bulgarians, the national awakening was handicapped by the dominance of Greeks in religious and cultural spheres. Nonetheless, nationalistically oriented middle classes gained in strength, their faith in ultimate independence being nourished by Orthodox parish priests, by historians, and by other literary folk. Minor risings in the forties testified to the widening acceptance of Bulgarian nationalism. The irresistible flow of history foreshadowed the liberation of all the small Balkan nationalities in the decades that lay ahead.

The Empire of the Tsars

It has already been shown that imperial Russia attained primacy in the high politics of Europe in the forepart of the nineteenth century. Here was an immense realm covering eastern Europe, stretching over northern Asia, and by way of the Aleutian island chain ending up in Alaska. What was the nature of the social structure of the empire of the tsars—very much "a riddle wrapped inside an enigma" for even informed westerners?

"Is it fair," inquired a Briton visiting the tsardom at

this time, "to make a comparison between the Russians and European nations which have been civilized and polished for many centuries? All will reply in the negative." Just below the Russian imperial household was the court aristocracy owning large estates, opulent palaces in city and country, kept up by hosts of servants, and frequently equipped with facilities for drama and orchestra. Inferior nobles held to the seclusion of their modest country "nests." In this privileged caste current French notions of refinement and courtly manners blended with crude customs inherited from the Russian past. For many an aristocratic household, life resembled a merry masquerade, replete with parties, balls, hunting, gambling, and kindred diversions. Said a memoir writer, "the winter was one perpetual carnival in Moscow." To the upper layer of the nobility, Tsarina Catherine II had imparted her own fondness for luxury, her insatiable passion for grandeur in architecture and for collecting art objects.

It was not unusual to find libraries well stocked with the works of the French *philosophes,* Voltaire above all, and on a narrower scale British and German authors. Children were tutored by French or Swiss masters, some of whom taught the rational and related notions of the Enlightenment to their charges. A few young nobles drifted to Paris or another repository of western culture to pursue studies.

Serfs comprised something like nine out of ten of the tsar's subjects. Most of them lived on estates of the nobility as farmers, craftsmen, or household domestics; the rest worked on crown properties. Enterprising landlords operated mills or mines, though little was known about the enormous natural wealth hidden beneath the earth. Soilworkers toiled laboriously during the growing season and hibernated throughout the long months of winter. In the event of a calamity of nature, landlords were expected to care for families on their properties. On the other side, it was permissible for owners to exchange, sell, or mortgage their serfs, or to punish the refractory even by banishment to Siberia. As described by Count Leo Tolstoy in *War and Peace,* grandest of historical novels and set in the era of Napoleon, relations between patriarchal masters and their serfs were normally humane; cruelty, while not unknown, was the exception. Occasionally, a capable serf blossomed out as an architect or a professional musician, or engaged in a business pursuit.

Their lives bounded by narrow horizons in thousands of small villages (*mirs*), without any book learning or meaningful cultural opportunities, the *"mooshik* millions" (serfs) led simple existences. They adored Mother Russia, as had been impressively demonstrated in the epic struggle with Bonaparte, venerated the tsar as a benevolent father, and at least two-thirds of them worshipped in the Orthodox state church.

Many ordinary folk in the tsardom were not Russian in nationality, for the empire contained Poles and Lithuanians, Finns and minority stocks on the southern rim of the Baltic Sea, Jews, Ukrainians, and Germans settled in the valley of the Volga—if they may reasonably be classified as distinct national groupings. Out in the Siberian vastness and in Alaska dwelt dibs and dabs of primitive Oriental peoples.

Not all the subjects of the tsar were communicants of Orthodoxy. There were variegated native religious sects and cults, as well as Uniate Catholics, Roman Catholics, Jews, Moslems, and some Protestants (pages 111, 116). For Orthodox churchmen it was a sacred duty to combat and convert these deviators from the national norm.

For commercial and naval purposes, Peter the Great had secured "a window on the Baltic," and he bequeathed to his successors an ambition to obtain a similar "window on the Mediterranean." Growing exports of grain, timber, industrial rawstuffs, and furs to the west of Europe enhanced the importance of the Turkish Straits. Increasing commerce and industry enlarged the middle classes, often the men forgotten by writers on Russian history. Some manufacturers possessed big mills by any contemporary standard, but most non-agricultural production was carried on in small shops or in serf huts. Prospering Russian merchants traded with foreigners and in home markets.

At the outset of the nineteenth century, the empire of the tsars boasted only two substantial cities, Moscow and St. Petersburg (Leningrad), each with approximately a quarter million inhabitants. A popular saying taught that traditional, semi-Oriental Moscow was the soul of Russia, while westernized St. Petersburg, looking to the future, constituted the national head. Recurrently the victim of devastating fires, the worst of all when French soldiers thrust into the community in 1812, Moscow impressed travelers from abroad as in reality a collection of villages. Its very heart was the famous Kremlin (or Citadel), extending over a hundred acres, chock full of religious and secular structures, and encircled by towering walls of pale pink brick. Reconstruction proceeded rapidly after the ruinous fire of 1812, and the city regained its reputation for the making of textiles, china, glass, leather wares, and fur garments. Back in 1755, Russia's first university had been organized in Moscow, and in the post-Waterloo decades it became a hive of intense intellectual activity.

As desired by Peter I, St. Petersburg had grown swiftly from an isolated fortress and trading post, into a splendid European-type community and a thriving commercial center, to the detriment of Archangel on the Arctic Ocean and Riga on the Baltic Sea. Normally ice-bound for about a third of each year and cursed with an unhealthy climate, St. Petersburg, nevertheless, attracted throngs of foreign traders, principally Germans and Britons.

As the capital of the sprawling empire, St. Petersburg was the headquarters of the large official class, as well as a home for learning and industry. Spacious buildings were erected (pages 134–135) while Alexander I reigned, to accommodate administrative, cultural, and business interest. Good taste in city planning was reflected in a regulation that the height of structures on Nevsky

Prospekt, the magnificent main thoroughfare, must not exceed the width of the street.

Other cities having more than local importance were Kiev on the Dneiper River, the metropolis of the Ukraine and famed for its ecclesiastical treasures, and Odessa, a bustling young shipping community on the Black Sea. All these urban centers contained, of course, contingents of propertyless workers, some of them freemen but perhaps more in servile status.

The Reign of Alexander I

This—or something like this—was the Russia over which Alexander I, only twenty-three years old, became emperor in 1801. His father Paul I, neurotic if not demented, was slain by a conspiratorial band, in which the heir-apparent participated. Alexander had not wished the tsar to be murdered; the nightmare memory of the crime tortured his mind and in the end may have unhinged it. Contemporaries and biographers of Alexander I have diverged sharply on the character of the man, on what he desired to do as emperor of all the Russias, and why. Alexander Pushkin, most renowned of Russian poets, called him, "the Sphinx who took his riddle with him to his grave." The tsar was incapable of pursuing a consistent line of thought, commented Prince Metternich of Austria.

The Russian autocrat wielded unlimited authority, backed by a submissive nobility, a ramified bureaucracy —secret police agents and spies included, an obedient Orthodox clergy, and loyal fighting services. Only the court aristocracy could exert any effective restraint upon Alexander's power. Progressive, liberal affirmations for which Alexander became widely known were seldom implemented by appropriate action. More than once, for instance, he promised to publish a constitution for the empire; in 1818 he declared that "he hoped to extend free institutions to all countries under my care." On his instructions. written instruments of government were actually drafted, only to be tucked away in an imperial drawer.

Paradoxically, Alexander granted the Polish kingdom, which was called the Congress kingdom, a remarkably liberal constitution for the time. Under its terms, deputies of the *Seym* or parliament were partly chosen by Poles on a broader franchise than in Great Britain or France. The kingdom was given considerable civil liberty and allowed to raise its own army. Friction between nationalistically minded Poles and the crown, however, turned so acute that the parliament was temporarily closed in 1820, and freedoms were whittled away.

Alexander I was aware of the iniquity of serfdom and familiar with its disadvantages. Late in the eighteenth century, bold Russian voices, influenced by Enlightenment doctrines, had declaimed against the "peculiar institution" of serfdom as symptomatic of national backwardness and inefficiency. If anything, agitation for emancipation increased in the Napoleonic era. "With God's help," the tsar publicly announced at Paris in 1814, "serfdom will be abolished in my lifetime." What happened? A law of 1808 prohibiting the sale of serfs was reaffirmed, and soilpeople in the Baltic provinces, not Russians in nationality, but Estonians and Letts, were set free (1816–1819) but not assigned any land. Consequently, liberated families labored on the property of soulless barons of German stock.

An atmosphere of comparative intellectual freedom reigned in Russia until about 1819. Ideas of western origin were tolerated, foreign books were admitted, and permits to travel abroad were not difficult to procure. Then the pendulum swung to restriction and restraint. The murder of Alexander's special agent in Germany, Kotzebue (page 43), profoundly disturbed the tyrant. And the mutiny of a guard regiment in 1820 led Alexander, coached by Metternich, to believe that a general conspiracy against the Romanov throne was being planned. Stiff regulations curbed the circulation of publications of every description and the curricula of institutions of learning were overhauled, courses thought to contain political dynamite being dropped in favor of more thorough instruction in religion.

Thereafter, the emperor, immersed in international politics which earned him the dubious sobriquet of "gendarme of Europe," neglected domestic affairs and spent a good deal of time traveling aimlessly around the empire. So much public power was vested in his confidant, Count Aleksei Aracheev (1764–1834), that he was tagged the "vice-emperor."

As minister of war, Arakcheev had proved a hardworking, thrifty, and even honest administrator, qualities rarely found in policymaking imperial officials. But so brutal and course was he that critics nicknamed him the "bulldog." Under the guidance of this inhuman martinet a network of "military colonies" was formed in 1816, suggestive, up to a point, of the labor "corrective" camps of Soviet Russia. Soldiers and their families by the tens of thousands were herded into the colonies, where, under rigorous discipline, they spent their waking hours in military drill, at work on the soil, or in shops. Since each settlement was designed to be self-sustaining, the imperial autocrat commanded large fighting forces at minimum cost. Small wonder that the settlements occasioned suspicion and consternation in other European countries. Quite likely, material conditions in the colonies were a shade better than in a typical Russian village, but recurrent disorders testified that all was not well. Yet this odious institution existed for two solid generations.

More and more, the crown bore heavily on Alexander's mercurial head. Melancholia stole upon him. The crowned "Hamlet" talked repeatedly of abdicating and even of emigrating to America in the company of a seductive Pole. In 1825, just short of forty-eight, death overtook him, though reports kept bobbing up that he had in fact run away so that he could live out the rest of his days in privacy and peace.

Episode in December

The passing of Alexander I presented anti-tsarist revolutionaries an unusual opportunity to stage small-scale
uprisings against the established system. Officers who
fought Napoleon or served in the occupation of France
came into contact with conceptions of the good life
alien to the Russian heritage. Men who had seen Paris
were never quite the same again. To change conditions
in Russia drastically, to translate ideas of freedom,
equality, representative government, and fairness into
realities, the anti-tsarists organized secret societies and
literary and debating clubs, and studied conspiratorial
methods employed by western insurgents such as the
Italian *Carbonari*. As occasion permitted, they spread
seditious sentiments among discontented soldiers.

Princes of the most aristocratic blood, affluent landlords, as well as military men lower in the social scale
joined the anti-tsarist rebels. Altogether they represented, however, only a tiny rivulet of thought and
feeling in the vast Russian ocean. Two main groups
emerged, one in the south being headed by a youthful
colonel, Paul I. Pestel (1793–1826). A voracious reader
who had adopted George Washington as his private
patron saint, Pestel advocated a republic with manhood
suffrage, the abolition of class privileges, and the liberation of the serf millions to whom land taken away from
the big proprietors would be allotted. Whole-souled
Russian nationalist that Pestel was, he wished the non-
Russian minorities to be forcibly assimilated.

The second leading clique centered in St. Petersburg and Moscow. Objectives there were not sharply
defined, some members favoring a limited monarchy on
the model of Bourbon France; it was generally understood that Russia's "peculiar institution" must be wiped
out, though no consensus was reached on the vital issue
of land for the freedmen.

For nearly a decade, plots to kill Alexander I, as his
father had been slain, had been eagerly concocted and
then abandoned. Since the tsar died without a legiti-

mate child, the crown should have passed to his brother, Constantine, but he had renounced his right in favor of a younger brother, Nicholas. Confusion and uncertainty persisted until Nicholas, who was detested as a harsh commander, was officially proclaimed tsar.

Ostensibly, as champions of the cause of Constantine, revolutionary-oriented officers incited military troops quartered in St. Petersburg to rebel. Since the strike against the autocracy occurred in December of 1825, the plotters came to be known as the Decembrists. "Constantine and constitution" served as the battle cry—the illiterate, serf soldiers wanting Constantine, their leaders, constitution.

From his cozy quarters in Vienna, Metternich exclaimed, "All Europe is sick of the same disease. . . . We shall learn that secret societies have been mainly responsible." Sharp street-fighting in St. Petersburg, observed by thousands of spectators, lasted only a few hours and stopped abruptly when Nicholas I ordered "a whiff of grapeshot" discharged against the mutineers. Southern revolutionaries staged an equally futile outbreak. Without mass support of the soldiers, without resolute leadership, the Decembrist outbursts were bound to fail. Ideas can be weapons, assuredly, but weapons can stifle ideas. It is a distortion to speak of the Decembrist affair as a revolution; it was too limited for that. It was an episode, hardly a chapter in the story of rebellious Russia.

Arrested ringleaders were tried by drumhead courts. Five men, Pestel among them, were hanged, and scores were banished to hard labor in bleak Siberia or in the Caucasus provinces. Years of apathy followed on the heels of the ruthless repression of the Decembrists.

Yet an aura of martyrdom came to surround the aristocratic participants in this first instance of an organized political insurrection in modern Russian history. Their deeds inspired many an unorthodox Russian man of letters, and created an anti-tsarist tradition of heroic proportions that proved of permanent importance.

In time, the events of 1825 affected unhappy intellectuals, who comprised the principal component in the thin red line of radical thought and behavior in the empire of the tsars. It was Nicholas Lenin, founding-father of Communist Russia, who declared, "The Decembrists awakened Herzen [an anti-tsarist intellectual of the next generation] and Herzen started the revolutionary agitation." Soviet schoolbooks hailed the disorders of 1825 as the source of the stream that culminated in the Bolshevik *coup d'état* of 1917, and lauded the well-to-do conspirators of December as model patriots, worthy of emulation.

The Passing of the Bourbons

King Charles X of France, who succeeded to the throne upon the death of his brother in 1824, was not without popular backing at his accession. Young Victor Hugo saluted the new ruler in warmly enthusiastic verses. But vague attachment to Bourbon royalism was rapidly dissipated. A libertine turned saint, believing he was divinely ordained to rule, the last of the Bourbon kings fraternized only with die-hard aristocrats, and disdained the upthrusting, assertive middle classes. The faults and follies of the vain and stupid Charles X soon rendered his kingship intolerable to broad layers of the French public.

Anticlericals resented the obsequious attitude of the king toward churchmen, witnessed by the pompous ritual of anointment when he assumed the crown, and by the increase in the number of bishops. They resented, too, the virtual monopoly on education, not excluding the right to intervene in universities, granted to churchmen. Though few Frenchmen took part in parliamentary elections or debates, hosts of non-voters scrupulously followed what went on in the lawmaking bodies. Loud outcries, for example, greeted the enactment of legislation authorizing compensation to landowners who had lost property during the great Revolution. Small gentry obtained little benefit, though large sums accrued to wealthy aristocrats, such as the Marquis Marie J. de Lafayette, whose teen-age heart had once been enrolled on the side of New World revolutionaries.

To satisfy state financial requirements, rates of interest on government bonds were scaled down, which alienated bourgeois investors; and many a peasant landholder feared lest his acres might be confiscated and returned to their pre-revolutionary owner. Unrest was aggravated by a slowdown in business starting in 1827, which meant "hard times" for many city workmen; manufacturing interests demanded higher tariffs as protection against British competition. Partisans of Bonaparte clamored for greater national grandeur than the Bourbon regime was producing.

The unpopularity of the regime of Charles X was openly demonstrated in 1827 during a review of the bourgeois National Guard. By way of retort, the crown clamped an effective gag on the press and dissolved the National Guard, known popularly as "the army of the people." Such attempts to reassert royal authoritarianism led Metternich to dispatch counsels of caution to Paris, and liberal-minded French churchmen attacked the crown with increasing shrillness.

Momentarily, in 1828, the monarch seemed to have taken a new tack, for his hand-picked ministry pushed through laws that were too liberal for conservatives and too conservative for friends of change. That moderate cabinet was soon—and stupidly—supplanted by another headed by Prince Jules de Polignac, a confirmed opponent of representative government and a blind exponent of absolutism. He was persuaded that the Holy Virgin had in fact selected him to save France from chaos!

Polignac pursued public policies that could scarcely have been carried through without the application of physical force. Early in 1830, the Chamber of Deputies was disbanded, and before a new election was con-

ducted, the king, seeking to shore up royal prestige and
to divert minds from home concerns, sanctioned preliminary measures to conquer pirate-infested Algeria.
The campaign started off auspiciously, though not
many voters were affected, for a large anti-Bourbon ma-
jority was returned.

Whereupon, Charles X decided upon bold action,
subversive of the constitution and of civil liberties. By
law, the crown was entitled to issue royal ordinances
with full force of law if an emergency existed. On
July 26, 1830, three such arbitrary decrees were published, dismissing the recently elected Chamber, re-
vising the electoral law in a manner to benefit arch
royalists, and restoring press censorship.

Paris exploded. One by one public buildings were
captured by the rebels, and troops ordered to suppress
insurgents fraternized with them. Never notably capable as a public leader, Lafayette took command of the
resurrected National Guard. After three days of desul-
tory street-fighting, Charles X set off for healthier
climates abroad, and the revolutionary leadership offered the crown to Louis Philippe, Duke of Orléans
and cousin to the deposed Bourbon. Promising to rule
as a "citizen king," the duke accepted; and the long
Bourbon ascendancy in French politics came to an
abrupt close. The July events produced important repercussions elsewhere in Europe as well as in France.

Summary

After Napoleon had been disposed of and peace settlements had been hammered out, Europe entered upon
a time of convalescence. Conservatism and stability
dominated public affairs. Even so, two novel and trans-
forming forces were at work. From revolutionary
France, the new Europe inherited the gospel of liberalism, meaning specifically constitutions, popular participation in government, civil freedoms, and visions of
national consolidation. These aspirations produced con-

vulsions from Lisbon to St. Petersburg. Small Serbian and Greek states took their places on the map. Disorders, inspired by liberalism, rose to a climax in 1830 when Paris caused a switch in dynasties and set rolling a fresh wave of outbreaks at other points on the Continent.

In the second place, a more subtle, a more dynamic revolution—industrialism—made a modest impact upon France, Belgium, and western Germany especially. From its English homeland, the making of goods by power machinery—call it machinofacture—spread onto the Continent. That trend accelerated the decline of the traditional regime dominated by the aristocracy and the advance of a bourgeois-individualist society.

True enough, the vast mass of Europeans still derived their livelihood from the soil. True enough, transportation was still negotiated by cart or carriage, stagecoach or sailing vessel. True enough, banking and other institutions of finance capitalism possessed hardly more than an elementary character. But more than mere germs of the age of machinofacture were already evident. With growing commerce and industry, even in central and eastern Europe, the middle classes gained in affluence and influence. Simultaneously, the propertyless workers in city and town, the proletariat, increased in numbers.

Except in the empire of the tsars, it was the bourgeoisie who furnished the impetus for remodeling governmental patterns on the style that had evolved over the centuries in Great Britain. Where national disunity existed, the middle-classes, more particularly the intellectuals, likewise carried the torch for national independence.

C H A P T E R . . . 3

The Gathering Storm

A July Kingdom Comes

Upon learning of the Paris revolt of 1830, Prince Metternich professed great dismay. "My life's work is destroyed," he cried in agony of spirit. Tsar Nicholas I feared that the flames of insurrection would spread eastward. Actually, the events of July inspired major upheavals only in Belgium and Russian Poland, and lesser risings at other points on the Continent. The new and moderate government of King Louis Philippe showed no interest in foreign adventure and solemnly pledged that revolutionary doctrines would not be exported. Never was there much danger of intervention from outside to restore the legitimate Bourbons; the sympathetic posture of the London cabinet toward the July monarchy would doubtless have frustrated an effort of that character. Presently, Metternich calculated—or hoped—the July regime would plunge France into civil strife. His eastern diplomatic associates promised cooperation if the French should threaten to extend political activity beyond their own borders.

Under the new dispensation in France, the constitution of 1814 was slightly altered. The crown was deprived, for instance, of authority to issue ordinances, as Charles X had done; fundamental civil liberties were set on firmer foundations; and qualifications for voting were slightly lowered. About three percent of the adult males were declared eligible to exercise the franchise, a limitation that infuriated militant proponents of universal manhood suffrage. The flag of the July monarchy carried the colors of the great Revolution—blue, white and red—and a spirited Gallic cock superseded the Bourbon fleur-de-lis on the insignia of the armed forces.

Called the last of the enlightened despots, King Louis Philippe wished to find and follow a golden mean in public policies, as necessary for national stability. He spoke of himself humbly as the "citizen king" and he bid eagerly for that fickle goddess, popularity. He was a child of the Enlightenment, a deist in religion, and reasonably virtuous in his private life. By reason of his exile during the great French Revolution, part of which he spent in the United States, the king possessed exceptional, firsthand knowledge of the western world. Dignified and amiable though he was, his pear-shaped head and his habit of appearing in public with a green cotton umbrella and a stiff frock coat made him an ideal target for the waspish pens of unsympathetic caricaturists.

For all his intelligence, Louis Philippe lacked the wisdom to keep his tongue in check. Immensely wealthy himself, he leaned heavily upon the moneyed plutocracy and the professional and managerial classes for political backing. Throughout his reign, France was fairly well off economically, and the country remained at peace with the world outside, save for a colonial war in Algeria. Yet, several attempts were made to kill him, and the National Guard frequently went into action against Bourbon legitimists, Bonapartists, republicans, and lesser antagonists.

Though the July monarchy has been indicted as a "do-nothing" government, the charge fails to stand up. Debates in parliament ranged widely and were conducted with vigor. The king, not a good judge of men, customarily picked conservative ministers, and, for demonstrated incompetence, they were upset with exasperating regularity. In the late thirties, Adolphe Thiers (1797–1877) and François Guizot (1787–1874) energetically competed for the prime ministership which contributed to cabinet instability. Both men had built up reputations as historical writers, both believed in constitutional government, but whereas Guizot contended that the crown should share directly in decision making, Thiers insisted that the king should "reign but not govern."

Thanks to press freedom, newspapers flourished, notably in Paris. Improvements in printing techniques facilitated the appearance of the cheap newspaper, such as *La Presse* in 1836; it published political and financial news and views, carried chapters from novels, and prospered on advertising. Because newspapers attacked the person of the king in offensive language and cartoons, restrictions on freedom of the press were in time imposed. In 1840 the famous Havas news-gathering agency started on its career with pigeon carrier service to London and Brussels.

On another front, the colorful French Foreign Legion was put on a solid footing in 1831. Soldiers of many nationalities were recruited and set to work finishing the conquest of Algeria. Subjugation of inland tribesmen proved an arduous task, not completed until 1847; the flag of France flew over Algeria until 1962. For French officers and the army rank and file, north Africa provided a convenient training ground.

Under state auspices, a considerable program of internal improvements was carried out. Apart from about 1,200 miles of canals, roads and bridges were bettered to the unmistakable gain of the rural population. More significant, the first railway tracks were laid in the late 1830's, using British capital and rolling stock. In a few years the monarchy experienced a boom in rail construction, and in 1842 a master plan was adopted to provide for a network of tracks extending from the focal point of Paris to the frontiers. Strategic as well as commercial considerations determined the routes that rail lines took. While at the outset some railways were built with private capital, the state acquired an ever larger share in ownership. Steam-powered ships appeared simultaneously with steam-driven locomotives.

Despite repeated recessions, machinofacture progressed steadily. The introduction of British machinery and factories transformed the making of cotton goods; but other textiles, such as wool and silk, were still turned out in small shops by traditional methods. That custom prevailed, too, in production of iron wares; the large factory was exceptional in the French economy. With the Paris branch of the House of Rothschild in the vanguard, banking and credit institutions grew rich and powerful.

Wealthy bourgeoisie exerted a dominant influence upon public affairs and modestly patronized the arts and letters. The intellectual champion of the middle classes, Professor Guizot expounded a philosophy of the divine right of the bourgeoisie to rule. The business community wished the scope of government kept at a minimum and supported an unadventurous foreign policy. Take this set as a whole—it was noted for greed and callousness as well as gossipy salons and parsimony, all of which was described in lush detail by the novelist Balzac (page 125).

The French population moved upward in number, the gains being largely urban, and by mid-century, Paris passed the million mark. Wageworkers in shop and mill, in commerce and communications, toiled long hours for wretched pay. The underprivileged of Paris, existing on a meagre diet of bread and potatoes, indulged in a good deal of sexual promiscuity and drunkenness; mortality rates ran high. These conditions, denial of the right to vote, strict discipline in work-shops, and installation of laborsaving machinery fed social discontent in town and city.

Although trade unions were unlawful and strikes were treated as sedition, not a little industrial warfare broke out, violently at times. Troops suppressed worker demonstrations. The silk-making city of Lyons wit-nessed bitter strikes in 1831 and 1834 which were broken only with considerable loss of life. As will be sketched later, a remarkable array of blueprints for wide-ranging social reformation was drafted in Paris, but the July monarchy, in keeping with the economic philosophy of *laissez faire,* paid little attention to the evils that afflicted wage earners. It is true that legisla-tion restricting employment of women and children was adopted in 1841, but since no inspectorate system was created, the law was flagrantly evaded.

Independent Belgium

It may be recalled that the Vienna settlement of 1815 united Belgium to the kingdom of the Netherlands in spite of differences in language, historical traditions, and religious affiliation. Friction between politically active Belgians and the Dutch authorities was con-stant, revolving around political rights, economic in-terests, and church questions. Though Belgium pos-sessed no natural frontiers, something akin to national consciousness developed.

On the morrow of the Paris rising of 1830, patriots in Brussels rebelled and declared the independence of their country. Belgium was proclaimed a parliamentary monarchy on the pattern of Britain, though with a wider voting public. Dutch troops proved incapable of beating down the insurgents, and with troubles at home, the eastern monarchies declined to send troops to suppress the insurrection.

In Belgian circles, considerable sentiment favored union of the little country with France, or at least a French prince as sovereign. On grounds of security, the

British ministry vetoed those ideas, but called a conference of ambassadors in London to decide the destiny
of Belgium. It was agreed in 1832 that Belgium should
be detached from the Netherlands; a German prince,
Leopold of Saxe-Coburg, who had personal ties with
both Britain and France, was installed as king.

It was not until 1839, however, that the Dutch government formally acknowledged the independence of
Belgium. At that time, the great powers guaranteed the
territorial integrity of the little state and promised, on
the insistence of Britain, that it should be permanently
neutral. The latter commitment at its inception was
pointed against France, and it stood inviolate until the
invasion of Belgium by the German armies in the early
days of the First World War.

Blessed with strong traditions of excellence in the
manufacture of textiles and with large coal reserves,
Belgium moved ahead rapidly in industry and mining.
Partly to free the country from dependence on Dutch
transportation facilities, a splendid railway system was
constructed by the government, and Belgium advanced
to front rank in the new age of machinofacture. It was
unfortunate, however, that the population was split
linguistically. In the southern, more industrialized areas,
the Walloons spoke French, the language of the well-
educated, the government, and the army. To the north,
the tongue of the Flemings, akin to Dutch, prevailed.

Ferment in Italy

The July revolt in Paris spurred bands of Italian *Carbonari* to fresh revolutionary activity. Serious disorders
took place in 1831 in the Papal States; rebels of Bologna managed to set up a republic and moved troops
close to the "Eternal City." On invitation of the pope,
Austrian regiments smacked down the insurgents and
repressed small risings in neighboring principalities.
Once more the wave of revolt receded, though the tide
kept rolling on.

On the ruins of the discredited *Carbonari,* a new

revolutionary society, *Giovine Italia,* "Young Italy," was founded to overthrow governments and prepare the way for national freedom by propaganda and conspiracy. Its founder was a militant son of Genoa, Guiseppi Mazzini (1805–1872), romantic prophet of the *Risorgimento,* single-minded lover of liberty, teacher and inciter of rebellions and of angry young men in particular. "Without liberty," he taught, "there is no true morality." He felt it his sacred duty to kindle hatred of Austrian domination of the peninsula as the prelude to breaking the Austrian hold. An ex-member of the *Carbonari,* Mazzini perpetuated in Young Italy the rule of absolute secrecy and a good share of the mystic razzle-dazzle of the older organization.

To his Utopian confidence in the ordinary fellow, Mazzini joined fierce hostility to the church, which, he felt sure, was a dying institution and certainly a prime obstacle to national consolidation. He dreamed of an Italian republic with its capital the secularized city of Rome. To achieve this goal, his disciples promised to make whatever personal sacrifices that might be necessary and to live a Spartan existence. Mild-mannered though Mazzini was, his frank advocacy of assassination and insurrection as the means to his end made him the most feared European revolutionary agitator of his generation.

As punishment for a bold appeal in 1831 to the king of Piedmont to assume leadership in the movement for national liberty and unity, Mazzini was forbidden to remain in his homeland. Eventually, he settled in London where he fraternized with Continental revolutionary refugees and ceaselessly promoted his propaganda campaign. His followers, many of them young only in spirit, carried the gospel of unity from Venice to Palermo, and thus made a valuable contribution to the quickening of confidence in national freedom. Not a few perished in revolutionary outbreaks demonstrating their faith, hope, and valor. "The tree of liberty," wrote Mazzini, "grows stronger when watered by the blood of martyrs." Yet, as a promoter of rebellions, Young Italy was no more effective than the *Carbonari*.

Into the society was attracted a tough-textured, young sea captain, Guiseppe Garibaldi (1807–1882), whose very religion was a consolidated Italy grounded upon republican principles. His ability to inspire affection, even idolatry, and his fearless, untiring labors for the national cause made him in time a patriotic legend. In one local rising Mazzini and Garibaldi worked together, and when the effort dismally collapsed, the latter hastened to South America where guerilla fighting in the interests of freedom enhanced his prestige among Italian patriots. Mazzini resumed his exile in England, sending forth essays and inspirational letters by the bushel. Steadily, the volume of propaganda for a republic mounted and attracted a sympathetic reception from widening circles of articulate opinion in the Italian states.

While Young Italy grew to manhood, a second much more moderate group preached national freedom by means of a federation of states under the presidency of the pope. The philosopher of this program was a dynamic priest of Turin, Abbé Vincenzo Gioberti (1801–1852). Parting company with Mazzini, to whose society he had belonged, Gioberti also abandoned revolutionary radicalism in favor of gradualism. He disclosed his thinking in *Del primato morale e civile degli Italiani (The Moral and Civil Primacy of the Italians)*, appearing in 1843. Arguing that Italy had never been so respected as when papal authority was most extensive, he pleaded that national union under the pope would enable the country to carry forward her mission as a trail blazer in the ways of civilized living. Italy alone, he believed, was capable of leading all Europe into some desirable form of international solidarity.

Since the Gioberti agenda neither advocated a republic nor called for the overthrow of reigning princes, it appealed to friends of unity who disliked—even dreaded—the extreme and revolutionary temper of

Mazzini. Three years after the publication of Gioberti's massive book, the hopes of his followers soared when a popular, liberal-minded archbishop was chosen to occupy the chair of St. Peter.

This new pope, Pius IX (1792–1878), commenced his pontificate by releasing a thousand political prisoners from jail. This act elicited from an alarmed Metternich the wry remark that "God never grants amnesties"; warnings of the dangers implicit in reform measures flowed in a stream from Vienna to the Vatican. Nevertheless, the pope authorized the lighting of the streets of Rome with gas and the building of railways, innovations that were as repugnant to his austere predecessor as vaccination. An advisory council was created to consult on secular questions in the States of the Church; citizens of Rome were allowed to elect administrative officials; and the papal state entered into a customs union with Tuscany and Piedmont. But the pope rejected demands for a constitutional system and refused to endorse agitation intended to break the strangle hold of Austria on the peninsula. Bitterly disillusioned, friends of liberalism and of national fulfillment turned elsewhere for leadership.

In the meanwhile, industrialism had penetrated more deeply into the Italian states. Starting in the Naples area in 1838, railways were introduced; several lines were constructed in Piedmont whose sponsors had firsthand knowledge of what was happening in Britain and in France. Political discontent in the Two Sicilies, in Europe's deep south, whose Bourbon ruler was as corrupt and bigoted as he was tyrannical, flared up in a series of risings; as the sequel to outbursts at the beginning of 1848, the king published a constitution. That gesture heralded general revolutionary storms in Europe at the mid-nineteenth century.

The Course of German History

As in the Italies, so in the Germanies, the French July revolution had repercussions in the form of riotous demonstrations and agitation in the press. Princes of several of the smaller states sought to silence opponents by accepting constitutions. At Hambach, in the Rhine area of Bavaria, in 1832 a boisterous throng shouted for free institutions and German patriotism, which inspired Metternich to secure adoption of a second set of repressive laws on the Carlsbad model—stiffening censorship and police surveillance. Thereupon, a band of infuriated youths vainly attempted to seize control of Frankfurt, the seat of the Federal Diet. That body retorted by creating an inquisitorial commission which arrested and condemned hundreds on charges of "Jacobinism." Thousands of suspects fled abroad. It appeared that the cause of liberal progress had been effectively stifled.

Yet that was merely a superficial interpretation. That liberalism possessed deep roots in educated circles was shown in 1837 when the ruler of Hanover, an old-style traditionalist, revoked the constitution, whereupon seven highly respected scholars at the university of Göttingen balked at taking an oath of loyalty to the crown. Dismissed for their temerity, they became heroes of the liberal middleclasses overnight and obtained chairs at other German institutions of higher learning.

In the meantime, the pace of economic change in Germany had been considerably accelerated, and that trend had far-reaching consequences, as in other countries, on the social structure and on political attitudes. Well-to-do middle-class men manifested increasing aversion to things as they were and came to believe that money, not birth, should determine one's place in the social hierarchy.

Already the *Zollverein* (page 44) under Prussian leadership had lowered barriers to economic expansion and had imparted a stimulus to general business activity across much of German Europe. Steadily, in the face of enormous difficulties, the German states registered unprecedented progress and displayed greater maturity in their unavowed race to catch up with the west of Europe economically, and to capture a fair share of world trade. Between 1830 and 1848 the greater use of steam power and machinery in production, larger mining operations, and the advent of steam transportation on land and water had quickening effects upon the economy.

An influential exponent of economic growth was Friedrich List (1789–1846), a Württemberg politician and economist. During a long sojourn in the United States, he accumulated a small fortune and upon his return home became a vigorous advocate of higher tariffs to protect young industries from foreign competition and of railway construction. His *Das Nationale System der Politischen Ökonomie (The National System of Political Economy)*, of 1841 reflecting, up to a point, the impressions he gained across the Atlantic, probed deeply into the mainsprings of a nation's economic health and helped to bring on a boom in railways. By the end of the forties the German states boasted 3,800 miles of track, the largest network in Europe and nearly twice the extent of French lines.

Since railways required tracks, rolling stock, and coal, they stimulated several branches of the economy. Faster and cheaper communications speeded up trade and industry in general. Manufacturing, though handicapped by guild monopolies which interfered with innovations and enterprise, progressed notably in the Rhine districts and in Saxony. It was at this time that the Krupp iron concern, which grew into the largest private industrial empire of the world, commenced operations. It was also in this period that the immense coal resources of the Ruhr valley began to be mined on a major scale. The way was opening up for Prussian statecraft to build a German empire quite as much on coal and iron as on "blood and iron."

The transition to economic adulthood was neither smooth nor easy. A changing tempo and general working conditions provoked complaint and hostility from broad strata of the population. The characteristic social consequences of industrialism appeared in the German states as they had earlier in England and France. Introduction of laborsaving machines, for example, robbed handicraftsmen of employment; maddened linen-weavers of Silesia tried to arrest change by smashing machinery and damaging factories and dwellings of millowners. The misery of the workmen, their revolt, and its suppression by the military arm provided the stuff for a stirring drama *Die Weber (The Weavers)* by Gerhard Hauptmann.

The evils in German towns of low wages for long working days, of foul and congested dwellings, and of women and children employment matched conditions in the countries to the west. Interest in social reformation was aroused, and, among painfully marginal farmers, emigration overseas was encouraged. A radical editor in the Rhineland, where factories multiplied, was expelled for shrill expositions of the harsh lot of working-class men and women and for derogatory utterances about the Prussian royal house. This man, Karl Marx, would become the most effective of all anti-capitalist thinkers and writers.

Population statistics testified to the general economic well-being in the German states: they jumped from approximately 25,000,000 in 1814 to around 35,000,000 by mid-century. Dramatic increases in farm production kept pace with the greater number to be fed. But in the late forties, hard times befell the Germans, in city and in country. Yields of potatoes—the poor man's best friend—and grain dropped far below average; prices skyrocketed; and actual famine afflicted some districts. Business operations slacked off sharply, obliging governments to furnish bare necessities to the urban unemployed. The enforced pause in industrial expansion ended in 1847, and the economy was ready for an exuberant advance; yet dark memories of privation in the depression had bearing upon impulses to revolt in 1848.

In 1840, King Friederick William III of Prussia, a hardened partisan of absolutism, passed away. He had

counseled his heir, Friederick William IV, to oppose
resolutely a constitution for the kingdom, the most
populous in the German complex. In point of fact, the
new monarch was very much the visionary dilettante,
more concerned about the arts and philosophy than
about the stern requirements of state management.
Nevertheless, he approved acts allowing political exiles
to return home and relaxing restraints upon civil liberties, and he sanctioned the appointment of professors
known for their progressive thinking to university posts.

At the outset of the reign, nationalistic emotions
were churned up when controversy in the Near East
(page 96) raised the possibility of war with France. A
wave of patriotic enthusiasm swept the German states,
which was crystallized in the well-known anthem "Die
Wacht am Rhein." It was recognized that in the event
of an armed struggle, Prussia would necessarily be the
principal bulwark of German defense. Almost as swiftly
as it had arisen, the war scare subsided; yet it strengthened the case for Prussian ascendancy in German politics and had enduring consequences for national feeling. But the king set his face like flint against further
concessions to the liberal spirit.

It is true, nonetheless, that local Prussian diets, purely
decorative institutions, were convened from time to
time. In 1847, with the country in the throes of economic crisis, representatives of the provincial diets were
summoned to send representatives to a united Prussian
assembly. Almost all the delegates belonged to the
landed proprietor class. When the crown asked approval of a loan to finance railways, liberal spokesmen
presented their price for doing so. Boiled down, they
demanded in effect that the assembly should be converted into a parliamentary body to be called together
periodically and that it should be endowed with effective rights in the making of laws.

Varied opinions on the character of the Germany of
tomorrow prevailed in the liberal Prussian opposition.
Feeling was strong for action to consolidate the German

nation politically. Some wished a constitution modeled upon the British instrument, while a band of extremists desired a republic! All that was much too much for a king who had flatly declared, "Never will I allow a written document to come between God in heaven and this land . . . to rule us with its paragraphs and to take the place of the ancient and sacred loyalty." Before he was many months older—and wiser—Friederick William IV was obliged to eat these words, but for the time being the united assembly was dissolved.

Yet the meeting had two noteworthy merits. First, the issue had been openly and dramatically joined between friends of constitutional and parliamentary government for Prussia and proponents of the outmoded doctrine of the divine right of the king to rule. Second, the diet brought into the limelight individuals who were to share significantly in the subsequent course of German political development. Not the least of these men was a thirty-two-year-old, aggressive, staunchly royalist Junker grandee, Otto von Bismarck.

In other German states of the forties, agitation for change gathered strength. In Bavaria, for instance, the king had become infatuated with a seductive Spanish ballerina and intended to make her a countess. Mob disturbances broke out against the crown. Material distress, as has been indicated, facilitated the acceptance of notions of popular government, and, in Saxony notably, of anticapitalistic ideas. All over German Europe, affluent bourgeoisie kept calling for a legal voice in affairs of state.

By 1848, the forces of reforming change had gained considerable vigor in the German states in numbers and in prestige, in conviction and in commitment to the advancement of human rights. Years before, in 1834 to be exact, the popular German man of letters Heinrich Heine had predicted, "A drama will be enacted in Germany in comparison with which the French Revolution will appear a harmless idyll." That prophecy was not fulfilled in the tumultuous years of 1848–1849, when failure was ultimately written on efforts to translate liberal principles into realities of state. Indeed, nearly a century elapsed before Heine's speculation came true—and then in the malevolent form of the enthronement of Adolf Hitler and his Nazis.

The Hapsburg Realm

The rival of Prussia for supremacy in German affairs was Austria, the realm of the Hapsburgs, the special domain of Prince Metternich. It was a multinationality empire, and the rising surge of liberalism in its varied facets after 1830, say, seemed to endanger the integrity of the state. Austria "is the House of Lords of Europe," proclaimed Talleyrand in colorful accents; "as long as she remains intact, she can absorb the Commons."

At 1815, the crown of this highly centralized state rested on the brow of Emperor Francis I and would continue thus to rest for twenty years. Definitely a narrow-minded man of the old school—handsome, though, on horseback—he commanded widespread popular affection, even veneration. "Austria's fate," the anthem of the empire taught, "will forever be bound up with the Hapsburg crown." Loyalty to the crown constituted a vital bond of the state; so in general did the sophisticated and elegant landed nobility, the armed services, the Roman Catholic Church, and the bloated bureaucracy, in which the police must be reckoned. Civil servants kept the cumbersome imperial machinery turning, not too efficiently, to be sure, for they were overburdened with paper work, yet with a fair degree of impartiality and honesty.

An important instrument in maintaining the status quo and combating novelties was the court police and censorship presided over by Count Josef Sedlnitzky (1778–1855) and operated by a host of agents and spies. This bureau prohibited everything in printed form that was interpreted as detrimental to conventionality in morals and religion or hostile to the existing political and social systems. The rein was drawn hard and fast on institutions of higher learning and their students. Censorship was not airtight, however; scholarly works and costly foreign publications were seldom banned, and the rigor with which controls were enforced varied in accordance with the political climate.

A devout practitioner of paternalistic absolutism, Emperor Francis I once informed a delegation of schoolmasters, "I have no use for scholars, but only for good citizens. It is up to you to mold our youth in this sense. Who serves me, must teach what I order; who cannot do this or comes along with new ideas, can leave or I shall get rid of him." Such was the temper of the man who more than any other determined the shape of Austrian public policies.

For management of internal administration, the emperor relied chiefly upon Count Francis Anton Kolowrat (1778–1861), a Bohemian grandee of competence and diligence, enlightened, though in no precise sense a liberal. He possessed a knack for reconciling somehow a multiplicity of conflicting interests and wills. His forte was public finance, and that area of government presented a tremendous challenge, for huge debts had piled up by reason of the Napoleonic wars, and year after year state expenditures outran income. Obliging bankers, the Rothschilds and lesser firms, came to the rescue with loans to cover deficits.

Prince Metternich, as is already well known, directed Hapsburg foreign policy. His remark that he sometimes governed Europe but never Austria, contains kernels of truth. He had no taste for the routine of domestic administration nor sense of purpose for details of home affairs. In the image of critics, however, Metternich personified all that was wrong in the Hapsburg Empire. Because of his immense prestige, his views sometimes carried weight in decision making on internal questions, though not always. Scattered about the sprawling realm were many provincial diets, or local assemblies, dominated by the privileged elite, and restricted in function to administrative responsibilities. If these bodies were impotent politically, they, nevertheless, served as forums for expression of opinion. More than once, Metternich tepidly recommended that the assemblies should be empowered to send delegates to a central advisory council, but the proposals attracted little support, and the chancellor was never disposed to fight energetically for them.

Metternich summed up his philosophy of government on the home front this way, "The business of a government is to govern, to govern well, to govern wisely, to govern with due regard to the diversities of tradition among divers peoples, but always to govern." Not a bad approach, but could this logic be applied in the Hapsburg realm? The emperor usually respected suggestions proffered by Metternich, and advised his successor to heed his counsels, forgetting Kolowrat.

Agriculture was overwhelmingly the mainstay of the Austrian economy. Many large estates were worked by hired hands, or by serfs who owed payments in kind and in labor service to their masters. Other dues had to be paid to state and church. The authority of the nobility over the soilpeople in the Hungarian portion of the monarchy matched the situation in the empire of the tsars. In certain areas, free peasants carried on a subsistence type of farming. Except for cities such as Vienna, Budapest, Prague, and Milan, the material needs of the masses were satisfied in the locality—bread, wine, potatoes, occasionally meat, and homespun clothing. Wandering peddlers, weekly markets, and occasional fairs purveyed other consumers' goods. It was only in the 1830's that industrialism in the western sense started to make a substantial impact upon sections of the Hapsburg realm.

Hapsburg Peoples

Around a hard core of German-speaking subjects, the House of Hapsburg had built a broad empire of peoples by marriage, inheritance, and the fruits of war. It had made substantial gains in the Vienna settlement of 1815. Apart from Germans, the principal linguistic groups were Magyars, Croats, Slovenes, Slovaks, Italians, Poles, and Czechs. All manner of diversities distinguished the rainbow of national groupings in the multinationality empire.

The Magyar gentry and the small middle class of Hungary constituted the proudest and the most troublesome of the Hapsburg nationalities. Men of letters, historians, poets, and collectors of ballads excited memories of past grandeur and dreams of future glory in this golden age of Magyar literature. A veritable passion set in for anything and everything that was distinctively Magyar—costumes, dances, what not. And, despite the censorship and restriction on foreign travel, revolutionary doctrines of freedom and independence filtered in from the west.

Under the sway of these varied influences, the Magyar obligarchy compelled the Hapsburg sovereign to restore ancient and treasured privileges—above all, the Hungarian diet or assembly. After a lapse of more than a decade, this body was reopened in 1825, a concession to Magyar self-esteem that in itself encouraged an assertive national spirit. At meetings of the assembly, patriotic politicians expressed grievances against the Austrian crown and kindled hopes of a larger measure of freedom for the Hungarian kingdom.

By act of the assembly in 1840, Magyar supplanted the traditional Latin as the exclusive language of government. Preliminary moves were undertaken to dragoon smaller nationalities—comprising about sixty percent of the population—into forsaking their national heritages. Eager though Magyar nationalists were for liberty and freedom, they denied fundamental human rights to Croats and Slovaks, for example; that stand severely bruised the feelings of minority intellectuals.

Egged on by authorities in Vienna, small knots of intellectuals among these nationalities initiated national movements among their kinsmen, dwelling upon their own historical traditions, languages and literature, and peculiar folkways. Beginning on a cultural plane, these activities presently assumed political and social qualities as well. Insofar as they were able, awakened patriots fought Magyar denationalizing pressures.

Within the Magyar ruling class, moderate and extremist factions emerged. Heading the former was Count Stephen Széchenyi (1791–1860), belonging to the top aristocracy and a devoted Hapsburg loyalist. Visits to western Europe convinced him that very much was out of joint in his homeland. Through his voluminous writings, "the greatest of the Magyars," as he came to be called, promoted cultural improvements and pleaded for political and economic reforms, even advocating that the nobility should renounce the privilege of tax exemption!

Partisans of moderation were crowded into second place, however, by militant Magyar nationalists, led in time by the picturesque Louis Kossuth (1802–1894). Of lowly origins, partly Slovak, he pushed to the front as a lawyer, estate manager, and gifted writer and orator. One day his oratorical prowess would mesmerize vast audiences in England and America as previously in Hungary. Attractively written reports on the proceedings in the Hungarian assemblies and fiery editorials in the "liberal" newspaper *Pesti Hirlap* immensely heightened Kossuth's popularity among Magyar left-wingers.

On charges of treason against the Hapsburg realm, Kossuth was thrown into prison in 1837; during his confinement he acquired wonderful fluency in the English language, which later stood him in good stead. His jail term consolidated, moreover, his prestige as a national hero. Becoming a convert to the teachings of Friedrich List, he charged that Austrian policies prevented the progress of the Hungarian economy, and he launched a strikingly successful drive to get Hungarians to buy only goods turned out in their homeland. More and more, Kossuth's national agitation assumed the trappings of a crusade.

Violent, prideful denunciations of Hapsburg lordship alarmed the prim Austrophile, Széchenyi faction, which warned that Kossuth was leading the nation along the road to civil war—as in fact he was.

At the 1847 elections for the Hungarian assembly, the Kossuth party scored a sensational victory. Passionate though the leader was for national freedom, there were elements of cant in his outlook, for he stubbornly resisted concessions to the smaller nationalities. He did, however, favor taxation of the great landed proprietors and liberation of the serfs. Agitation for full home rule rose to a peak early in 1848 when information reached Budapest that Paris had rebelled and toppled the French king from his throne.

Among the Italian minority, concentrated for the most part in Lombardy and Venetia, the selfsame impulses of national awakening were at work as elsewhere in the peninsula. The government in Vienna prized its possession in Italy not alone as an economic and manpower asset, but because it stood as a potential barrier against France, and re-enforced Austrian mastery of the Adriatic Sea. Instruments of Austrian control included an elaborate administrative machinery and a network of advisory councils in which natives had a modest voice. Large garrisons of Austrian troops were ensconced in strong fortresses, ever-ready to overawe malcontents or to put down local nationalist outbreaks.

Young Italy spread revolutionary propaganda by word and deed, much anti-Austrian literature written by exiled patriots being smuggled into the provinces. More so in Lombardy than Venetia, conspiracies against Hapsburg lordship popped up spasmodically; captured rebels were sentenced to foul dungeons, from which they often emerged with haloes of martyrdom around their heads.

Apart from alien lordship, the obligation of young Italians to serve in the Austrian army, the prevalence of espionage, and the scale of taxes (seldom popular anywhere) evoked mingled grumbling and protest. On the other side, population figures moved upward, becoming a fifth of all Italians; institutions of learning improved somewhat; and the administration of justice, save for political culprits, was praiseworthy. Considerable layers of the citizenry, aside from the middle classes and city wage earners, gave evidence of being contented, if not downright Austrophile or disinterested in the flag that flew over them.

As the years of the forties drew out, however, national aspirations attained much wider popularity, aided by fresh impulses issuing from Rome after the enthronement of "liberal" Pope Pius IX. Agents of national unity from outside and literary agitators redoubled their operations. On the eve of the revolutionary tumult of 1848, cities and towns seethed with Austrophobe, patriotic emotions.

The city of Milan progressed economically, especially in the manufacture of silk and cheaper textiles, and was by way of becoming a key railway junction. Whatever its shortcomings, Austrian administration made Milan a gayer and safer place in which to live.

National fervor likewise increased among articulate Poles within and without the Austrian dominions. It may be recalled that in the Vienna settlement of 1815 the city of Cracow, the unique cultural and intellectual capital of the Polish nation, and the surrounding area had been formed into a free and independent republic. It abutted upon the Hapsburg province of Galicia, peopled partly by Poles, partly by Ukrainians (Rutherians), who cultivated the lands of the Polish nobility. Cracow served as an asylum for political refugees from dismembered Poland and as headquarters for agitation on behalf of national resurrection. In 1846, a rebellion took place in Cracow, intended to be the starting point for the revival of Polish independence. Polish landlords of Galicia solicited the help of the Ukrainian countryfolk in striking off the Austrian yoke.

This piece of audacity ended disastrously for the cause of Polish freedom. Austrian soldiers occupied

Cracow, and oppressed Ukrainians fought their Polish masters, killing many and destroying property. They balked at returning to the fields unless and until degrading feudal obligations were canceled. Austrian officialdom, calculating that acquiescence would invite soilworkers elsewhere to rebel, vetoed the Ukrainian demands. As for Cracow, with the assent of the Russian and the Prussian governments, it was merged with Austrian Galicia.

Of all the Slav-speaking nationalities, the Czechs were doubtless the most advanced materially and culturally. Their ancient kingdom of Bohemia had been added in 1526, like Hungary, to the possessions of the Hapsburgs. Early in the nineteenth century, the Czech national renaissance strode forward, promoted by the historical writings of Palacký (page 128) and the literary work of other patriotic intellectuals. As the foremost Czech personality, Palacký demanded that the Austrian nationalities be granted opportunities for self-fulfillment on the basis of equal rights. He wanted the Hapsburg Empire preserved, though, as a strong bastion against expansionist appetites in either Germany or Russia. In the forties, Czech nationalists intensified their attacks upon the Austrian bureaucracy, denial of civil freedoms, and heavier taxation.

An Era Ends

Among educated Germans of Austria and in student circles, dissatisfaction with prevailing institutions mounted in volume and intensity. Critics attacked the authoritarian government, vilified the censorship as an affront to human dignity and a brake on progress, and flailed away at inefficient and tyrannous bureaucrats—"thousands of little Metternichs," it was said. In the vanguard of the opponents to the status quo were Viennese clubs of liberally oriented professional men and a sprinkling of title bearers. Habitués of coffee-houses busily exchanged opinions on reforms that ought to be introduced. Spokesmen of Jewry demanded the removal of discriminatory regulations, while friends of rural interests called for the abolition of the feudal burdens borne by soilworkers. Try as they would, police and agents of the censorship could not stifle the cascade of ideas.

In the meantime, the coming of machinofacture, an upswing in coal mining, the laying out of railways, and the advent of steam vessels on the Danube and in sea-going trade, yielded the same social results in Austria as in other European countries. Urbanization increased. Textile factories drove handicraftsmen out of business. Unskilled mill operatives worked and lived in misera-ble environments. Within the medieval walls of Vienna or out in the expanding suburbs, many families dwelt in fearfully overcrowded tenements or in hovels lining waterways. The enlarged bourgeoisie not only resented the social superiority of the noble class, but reproached churchmen because of their special privileges. Many wanted a constitutional and parliamentary government, in which they would have a positive say in the policies of the country, as well as guaranteed basic rights for all citizens.

Since Emperor Ferdinand I, who ascended the throne in 1835, was afflicted with an incurable malady, the management of state affairs was undertaken by an ill-assorted state council. Chaired by the very conservative Archduke Louis, this body contained Chancellor Met-ternich and Count Kolowrat. Personal feuds between these two statesmen made it difficult to get much done except routine business, and, by indirection, quarreling enheartened the advocates of liberalism.

Someone has aptly described the decade of the forties as "the death years of old Austria." A rising tide of political and social unrest swept over both the German-speaking population and the other peoples of the realm. Bad harvests and slackened activity in manu-facturing and trade brought destitution in town and country, and, therewith, heightening agitation for a "better deal." Elite aristocrats joined members of the Hapsburg household in agreeing that the symbolic and hated Metternich must go and that a constitution must be bestowed upon the country.

In this situation, news of a Paris revolution in 1848 was greeted by explosive violence. Citizens of Vienna and students, many of them as poor in purse as they were rich in revolutionary exuberance, demonstrated on the streets, shouting for the dismissal of Metternich, the "Dali Lama," to recall only a printable epithet. Circulation of a speech made by Kossuth in Budapest in which he demanded a parliamentary regime for Hungary and constitutional government for the whole Hapsburg Empire added fuel to the flame of insurrection. Under pressure from the imperial household, Prince Metternich, seventy-six now and weary in mind and body, grudgingly handed in his resigation. It is interesting to note that his downfall occurred ninety years to a day before the Nazi chieftain, Adolf Hitler, seized Vienna.

Even the revolutionaries were astonished at the ease with which the self-styled "coachman of Europe" was ousted from power. While the ex-chancellor traveled to a safe haven in London, a hurricane of rebellion raced across the cities of the realm. Hoping to check the anarchical storm, Hapsburg officials promised that a constitution would be forthcoming. An era of history closed abruptly.

The "Iron" Tsardom

"My greatest pleasure," Tsar Nicholas I remarked, "is to talk to my beloved soldiers, to know their needs, to assure myself of their training and progress—nothing interests me so much." Personally, he considered himself an expert in many branches of public affairs and culture, though when he visited the girlish Queen Victoria she wrote him off as an "uncivilized mind." He never tired of military parades and reviews; in 1839 he had the Battle of Borodino, in which Muscovites had fought the armies of Napoleon, reconstructed on the actual site of the bloody struggle, 150,000 soldiers acting parts. Military discipline and stern application of despotic power stand as hallmarks of a reign which on many counts set patterns in public administration that persisted until the Bolshevik seizure of control in 1917.

To forestall any likelihood of a repetition of the Decembrist outbreaks, which greeted Nicholas I upon his accession, he created a "third section" of the imperial chancellery, a new set of secret police. Charged with keeping the tsar and topflight officials informed on manifestations of subversion, the principal targets of the "third section" were unconventional men of letters. Their writings and their daily lives were kept under surveillance, their sense of intellectual adventure shackled as fully as possible; the same kind of scrutiny applied to foreigners, extending into their private correspondence. Scholarship and literature, it was intended, would be forced to conform to the official outlook, to the "party line" indeed.

Tsarist police failed, however, to ferret out all the opponents of the Romanov tyranny or their literary productions. As with the police, so in other departments of government the bureaucratic rolls increased greatly. Some cultivated ministers of state turned up, though few showed much gumption, and peculation was rife in all levels of the official class. As a step forward, the enormous mass of basic and administrative laws, court room procedures, and the like were boiled down to forty volumes, which served with only modest alterations to 1917. But gross venality and class inequalities in the administration of justice went unchanged.

Except for his Polish subjects, Nicholas I had no noteworthy trouble with non-Russian nationalities. Alexander I, it may be recalled, conferred upon Poles in the Congress kingdom the most enlightened constitution in Europe, with representative institutions, personal and religious freedoms, and an army. Dissatisfaction with Russian overlordship resembled the discontent that emerged in captive Poland after the Second World War. Deputies in parliament clashed angrily with tsarist agents, and dreams of revival of the old, broad, and independent Polish state would not be forgotten. Hopes of regeneration were kept green by patriotic writers, by Roman Catholic churchmen, and by secret societies, which enrolled thousands of members in Austrian and Prussian Poland as well as in the Congress kingdom. Literature assailed Russian domination in abusive terms. When Nicholas I submitted to formal coronation in Warsaw in 1829, his reception was extremely frigid.

The next year, the Paris revolution furnished the spark that set fire to the Polish powder keg. Military men and part of the army, aristocrats, mature intellectuals, and Warsaw students joined in the insurrection. Despite a papal admonition to obey the tsar in keeping with the precept "Render unto Caesar," certain churchmen inspirited the rebel forces. On the other side, the apathetic or war-weary countryfolk, wishing only to be left in peace, declined for the most part to shoulder arms. Not only was a brand new constitution fashioned, but the independence of Poland was jubilantly proclaimed. "Love for country, as it exists in a Polish soul," philosophized the Russian poet Pushkin, "has always been connected with death."

It was confidently expected that military assistance would be rendered by western Europe. But though there was considerable press support for the revolutionaries, western governments no more aided the Poles than they helped the Hungarian freedom-fighters of 1956. Without foreign aid, neither of these rebellions could possibly overwhelm the massive might of Russia. In addition, schism inside the Polish leadership over the objectives to be fought for grievously impaired the conduct of the fighting.

To stamp out the "infamous treachery," Nicholas I

ordered into Poland armies numbering better than
three times the rebel forces; many of the soldiers were
hardened veterans of recent campaigns against Turkey.
Nonetheless, the Poles gave a good account of themselves; they were aided by an epidemic of cholera which
decimated the troops of the tsar and ravaged wide sections of the Russian civilian population. Yet the eventual outcome of the struggle was never in doubt, and
in the summer of 1831, the Russian commander joy-
fully informed the tsar, "Sire, Warsaw is at the feet of
your Majesty!"

Straightaway Nicholas demonstrated that the nick-
name "iron tsar" was well chosen. Hundreds of rebels
were imprisoned, deported eastward, or put to death,
and the estates of insurgent magnates were confiscated.
Thousands fled to western Europe to plot another
rising, and a smaller contingent beat its way to the
United States where memories of 1776 and the participation of Polish volunteers in the War of American
Independence had not been forgotten. Looked upon as
martyrs for liberty, like the Hungarian refugees of
1956, the destitute newcomers, mostly soldiers as well
as lower nobility, were voted generous acreages in
Illinois by the U. S. Congress.

All the autonomous institutions of the Congress
kingdom were abolished, and the region was incorporated bodily in the empire of the tsars. On the edge of
Warsaw a large citadel was raised with guns in position
to overawe the city, parts of which were ringed around
with fortifications. These constant reminders of Russian domination were hated no less than the towering
Palace of Science and Culture erected in Warsaw by
Marshal Josef Stalin after the Second World War.

As features of a campaign to Russify the unhappy
Poles, Warsaw university and a fine school of engineer-
ing—spawning beds of patriotic impulses—were closed;
the Russian language was made obligatory in schools;
and a tight rein was drawn upon Catholic institutions

and churchmen. Sections of the press and theaters in western Europe and the United States showered abuse upon the tsar as the author of the brutal treatment of "crucified Poland," and in so doing they nourished an acute feeling of Russophobia.

Once the Polish nightmare had been blasted away, police authority in Russia was tightened, if anything The political creed of the realm was neatly summed up by the minister of education, Count S. S. Uvarov, a scholar with lively cultural tastes, as "Orthodoxy, Autocracy, and (undiluted Russian) Nationality." Observers from abroad remarked upon the regimentation in the empire of the tsar, the universal prevalence of terror and fear, of mass poverty and humility. "My great objection to this country," decided United States Minister James Buchanan in 1832, "is the extreme jealousy and suspicion of the government." In much the same vein a keen-witted French aristocrat commented in 1839, "One does not die, one does not breathe here, except by permission or by imperial order. . . ." The Russia of Nicholas Romanov had many conditions in common with the Russia of Nicholas Lenin.

Despite the "iron curtain" that the "iron tsar" raised round his empire, despite the "third section" whose members were as likely to be as lax as gimlet-eyed, intellectual ferment existed inside the small educated circles. Schools were scarce—not one conscript soldier in fifty was literate; enrollment at institutions of higher learning was very low; and the circulation of journals of opinion and scholarship was decidedly limited. And yet in close-knit student clubs at the University of Moscow (a "wolf's den" in official eyes), and in literary salons, youths and their elders discussed the ideas of German philosophers or the doctrines of French anticapitalist theorists without fear of espionage or betrayal. Books were smuggled into the country, and intellectually hungry youths were smuggled out. Russian literature experienced her finest hours in this era; a few literary critics circulated provocative notions about society and government.

From these sources two disparate schools of thinking on the past and the future of Russia—and much else relevant to heaven or earth—shaped up. As a general proposition, the entire intelligentsia reviled the tsarist censorship and the oppressive officialdom and wished to see the shackles stricken from the *"mooshik* (serf) millions." But one set, spoken of as the "westernizers," urged imitation of Europe, tended to agnosticism in religion, and poked fun at the Russian national heritage.

Pitted squarely against the westernizing sector of the intellectual elite were the Slavophiles, admirably personified by the versatile Aleksei S. Khomyakov (1804–1866). Acquainted with the West at firsthand, he made his name as a poet and dramatist, as a writer on theological themes, and subsequently as an editor. Many a Slavophile agreed that contemporary Russia was insufferable, but they begged to dissent from the sweeping generalization that the past was a blank sheet of paper.

Instead, Russia boasted a goodly inheritance and it would be a mark of wisdom to revive the institutions and customs that prevailed before the reforming zealotry of Peter the Great; with scant concern for historical accuracy, Slavophiles built up romantic, intriguing myths about old Russia. Far from borrowing from the West, Russia should follow unswervingly her own peculiar line of development. Deeply, even mystically attached to the Orthodox Church, Slavophiles repudiated anything verging on rationalism. And their secular faith had a Messianic tinge to it, for they held that the future belonged not to the decadent West, but to vigorous and unspoiled Russia, summoned to regenerate all humanity.

How, next, did Russia's "peculiar institution" fare while Nicholas I ruled? Sporadic local outbreaks of bondsmen hinted at the urgency of reform. Like his predecessor, the tsar appreciated that serfdom was a vicious malady, or in his own language, "serfdom is an evil; no one can have any doubts about this and every reasonable observer sees perfectly well that the present situation cannot continue. At the moment, even to think of the emancipation of serfs would be to aim a blow at public discipline. But a way must be prepared for the gradual passing over to another order of things."

On imperial order, committee after committee was instituted to study the problem from the grass roots and come up with the recommendations for a "new deal." Full investigation preceded action to alleviate somewhat the lot of the state or crown serfs: improved techniques of cultivation, better medical care, lower taxes, and modest revision in the recruitment of soldiers.

Yet landed proprietors, as a class, infuriated by these concessions, opposed intervention by government on behalf of the "mooshik millions" on their estates. On this question, the iron in the tsar's backbone deserted him. If he arbitrarily ordained liberation by ukase, he almost certainly would have precipitated civil disruption. Remembering doubtless that his father and grandfather had been murdered by aristocratic plotters, it seemed intelligent to let matters drift.

Growing urbanization in western Europe, meantime, heightened the demand for Russian grain and other soil products. Shipments in the forties bounded upwards; since plans to enlarge the merchant fleet failed of full implementation, goods moved in and out largely in western cargo carriers. The first railways were constructed and a few large factories, especially to make cotton goods, were added to the limited industrial resources.

Building of the principal trackage, connecting St. Petersburg and Moscow, commenced in the forties. The tsar drew on a map, it is said, an arrow-straight line between the two metropolises and fixed that course as the route. An American consulting engineer on the

project was an individual far less well-known than
Whistler's mother, namely Whistler's father. Funds to
pay for construction were partly borrowed from the
West; French and German capital aided in building
new mills, some of whose machinery was imported from
Britain.

Very bad transportation facilities militated against
commercial advance—handicapped army operations
too. River-shipping was cheap but quite inadequate,
and useless in winter months. Roads in the southern
provinces, where stone was scarce, were hardly better
than trails and were soggy after rainfall; bridges left
much to be desired. Nevertheless, foreign trade increased and, since a high proportion of commerce
passed through the Turkish Straits, concern in government quarters about the Ottoman Empire was
quickened.

The Eastern Riddle

The major powers of Europe, with a reservation in the
case of Prussia, manifested an active interest in the
Near East, in the Ottoman realm, so visibly on the
downgrade. Muscovite ambitions to win control over
Constantinople (Istanbul) and the adjacent straits—
"the keys to Russia's backdoor"—are as old as Tsar
Ivan the Terrible and as young as Josef Stalin. It was
the rooted conviction of Nicholas I that Turkey, which
he indelicately tagged "the sick man of Europe," stood
at death's portal. Unwilling to accept that diagnosis,
the British government thought its commercial and
imperial interests (India not least) dictated preservation
of the realm of the sultan. The main line of Chancellor
Metternich paralleled the British desire to maintain
the status quo. French policy lurched erratically from
amputation of territory to protection of the Ottoman
dominions.

Throughout the nineteenth century, the decline in
the strength and authority of Turkey and the conflict-

ing purposes of the leading European countries comprised prime elements in the explosive, trouble-yielding
Eastern question. There was yet a third consideration:
the aspiration of subject peoples—or their political
leadership—to break loose from Ottoman lordship.
That factor likewise operated in the 1830's.

Down in Egypt, a talented, assertive vassal of the
sultan, Mehemet Ali, dreamed ambitious dreams of
supplanting his master, and twice his designs threatened to bring the larger nations of Europe onto the
battlefield. In 1831, Egyptian armies invaded the province of Syria and advanced upon Constantinople. Not
having recovered from the 1828–1829 defeat by Russia,
Turkish troops offered only feeble resistance. At that
juncture, the sultan turned to the hereditary enemy—
Russia—for assistance, which arrived in the shape of
both naval and army contingents. The British cabinet,
upheld by anti-Russian sentiments which had been
aroused by the suppression of the Polish rebels and by
competitive imperialism in Central Asia, protested violently over the Russian intervention, and France joined
in the hue and cry.

The war scare subsided, however, when Mehemet
Ali, his purposes far from appeased, broke off the fighting in exchange for Turkish recognition of his authority over Syria. By way of reward for Russian assistance,
Turkey signed in 1833 the Treaty of Unkiar Skelessi—
ostensibly a pact of friendship and alliance. An unpub-
lished article obligated the sultan to close the Turkish
straits to all foreign warships upon the request of the
tsar. In effect, the Muscovites had converted the Black
Sea into their private lake. Altogether the diplomacy
of the tsardom had achieved a dazzling coup; for any
practical purpose, Turkey had been reduced to a pro-
tectorate of Russia, a captive puppet.

Only slightly less outraged than London, Metternich,
ever eager to recover for Vienna the central position in
the high politics of Europe that it had occupied in
1814–1815, attended in 1833 a summit conference with

the Russians at Münchengrätz in Bohemia. Participating, along with their chief ministers, were Emperor Francis I and Tsar Nicholas I, distrustful of Metternich whom he termed "an enemy of the human race." After detailed exchanges on international questions of mutual interest, the negotiators pledged themselves to maintain the integrity of the Ottoman Empire, and, if necessary, to act together to put down Polish revolutionaries. Since Prussia acceded to the understanding, the conservative eastern bloc was reconsolidated. Nicholas I looked upon his two allies as a protective screen against revolutionary impulses along his western border.

Seeking to regain the lost province of Syria, the sultan in 1839 ordered troops into the region only to have them routed. Once more Egyptian columns pointed for Constantinople. This time the "Concert of Europe" rallied behind Turkey, except for France which backed Mehemet Ali, who now demanded recognition as hereditary ruler of both Egypt and Syria. The French ministry, presided over by the adventuresome Thiers, wished both to build international prestige and to strengthen French influence in Egypt. Bellicosity flamed to white heat in 1840, and an armed clash between France, on one side, and the German states and Britain on the other seemed in the offing. However, pacific counsels carried the day; France toned down, obliging Mehemet Ali to modify his pretensions. He acquired for his family the title of ruler of Egypt in perpetuity, as a province of the Ottoman state.

Thereafter, in 1841, the great powers entered into a Straits Convention, closing the Turkish Straits to warships of all countries in peacetime. That important prohibition became part of the fundamental European law of nations. As for the Ottoman Empire, the sultan issued a fresh batch of wide-ranging reforms, but alas, they were scarcely worth the paper on which they were written. Erelong, the autocrat of all the Russias renewed pressure upon Turkey, which led into another chapter in the Eastern riddle—the Crimean War.

The July Monarchy—Last Phase

Prime Minister François Guizot dominated the French political stage in the last phase of the July monarchy. A scholar in politics, Guizot, like his king, failed to read the signs of the times and to press for remedies of political and social ills. Not only did he wink at—if not openly condone—the deliberate perversion of parliamentary institutions by bribery and corruption, but he uncompromisingly resisted broadening the right to vote. Tough to the end, he retorted to agitators for franchise reform "enrich yourselves"; that is, accumulate enough cash to pay the minimum tax necessary for the suffrage privilege.

Actually, the number of citizens who satisfied the tax requirement to vote increased to almost 250,000, plain evidence of the growth of wealth under the July monarchy. In the sphere of foreign affairs, the guiding principle of Guizot was "peace everywhere, always." Never a popular politician outside of the monied aristocracy, Guizot banked heavily upon political apathy to perpetuate his ministry. Royal pomp and pageantry suffered neglect.

Many an articulate Frenchman was bored. Many another wished for change in the pattern of government, or in economic institutions, or in social organization. The conduct of international policy, however judicious and realistic it was in fact, evoked bitter denunciations as too tame and timid. Specifically, proud Frenchmen resented the diplomatic retreat in the controversy over Mehemet Ali, who had generated a good deal of uninhibited French enthusiasm. When France yielded in an embarrassing dispute with Britain over who should marry whom in the royal house of Spain, Frenchmen blasted king and minister for supine submission to the island kingdom.

Spokesmen for the return of the Bourbon dynasty, for whom the July regime was "a profanation of monarchy," never ceased to rebuke the managers of state business. And to a generation more familiar with the glories of Bonaparte than with the unspeakable agonies his rule had caused, the "Napoleonic legend" made an especial appeal. Men of letters artfully embroidered and embellished the glamorous features of the career of the "little Corsican." On two occasions the legatee of that tradition, Louis Napoleon, prematurely raised the standard of revolt against Louis Philippe, and thereby quickened nostalgic memories of French grandeur while his uncle had been in power. Napoleon's booklet, *De l'Extinction du Paupérisme (The Extinction of Pauperism),* urging radical social reform, attracted the hearty applause of anticapitalist thinkers. Amidst tumultuous popular emotionalism, the corpse of the late emperor, accompanied by the king's own son, was transferred from St. Helena to Paris. Napoleon's elaborate tomb and the magnificent Arc de Triomphe advertised the Bonapartist cult.

Believers in manhood suffrage also lined up with the adversaries of the July monarchy. Resurgence of interest in political and social democracy was shown in one direction by the eager purchase of *De la démocratie en Amérique (Democracy in America),* a best seller by Alexis de Tocqueville. The author composed this classic after study of the United States on the spot during the administration of Andrew Jackson.[1] Though he personally dreaded popular government, de Tocqueville discovered a good deal in the New World democratic adventure that was admirable and worthy of emulation.

The republican idea marched hand in hand with the democratic; a host of antimonarchical clubs centering in Paris plotted revolutions to throw down the monarchy. Recurrent republican outbreaks were suppressed, but the faith prospered underground.

---

[1] "I sought there," the French aristocrat explained, "the image of democracy itself, with its inclinations, its character, its prejudices, and its passions in order to learn what we have to fear or to hope from its progress."

Novel Social Doctrines

Paris, the "City of Light," the historic hotbed of unorthodox speculation and revolutionary impulses, was
the headquarters of an exciting set of anticapitalist[2]
social theorists who disseminated their thinking in all
manner of publications and through societies devoted
to discussion and debate. Their creeds radiated across
the western world and their city became a mecca for
unconventional European thinkers. "I entered Paris as
men used to enter Jerúsalem or Rome," ecstatically
wrote Alexander Herzen, an engaging left-winger who
had been expelled from his native Russia.

Certain French thinkers, committed to optimistic
plans for social progress and against *laissez-faire* individualism, were called "Utopian socialists," and the
label stuck. After an adventurous career, the pioneer of
this school, Comte Henri de Saint-Simon (1760–1825)
came to the conclusion that the proper study of mankind was not man but the masses. So broad was the
knowledge of this eccentric and original philosopher
that Karl Marx bracketed him with the systematic
thinker Hegel (page 113), calling them the most encyclopedic minds of the age.

The terms industry, production, and organization
were central in the thought of Saint-Simon. "The
golden age of the human race is not behind us," he
cried, "but ahead of us. Our fathers will never see it,
our children will see it some day; it is for us to prepare
the way." In the idyllic new age, a Council of Newtons,
composed of scholarly scientists and socially dedicated
technocrats, would govern. Under their management,
the greatest advantages would accrue to the greatest
number. All privileges arising out of birth would be
canceled and the obligation to work would become
universal. By means of economic planning, the gnaw-

---

[2] "Anticapitalist" is preferable to the more ambiguous terms
"socialist" and "communist," which attained currency in the 1830's.

ing tension of competition and all kinds of exploitation would cease.

Voltairean skeptic though Saint-Simon was, repudiating the "divine order" of Christian theology, he nonetheless insisted that a religion, a Messianic secular creed, was necessary. His last and best known piece of writing, *Le Nouveau Christianisme (The New Christianity)*, asserted that the certainties of science would crowd aside the speculations of conventional religion. The lot of the most numerous and poorest stratum of society would be improved by application of the Christian precept of the comradeship of man.

Wild and woolly though the teachings of Saint-Simon seemed to sober-minded contemporaries, they won' a band of followers, who drafted blueprints for gigantic transportation and banking projects and organized a movement. They wished to capture governments and then shape them to the principles of Saint-Simon. For a time they imagined they had uncovered just the ruler to apply their schemes—in the person of Pasha Mehemet Ali! Their stand on the emancipation of women allegedly verged upon free love; and, they were accused of conspiring against the French kingdom. The government dissolved the cult, but the ideas of Saint-Simon fertilized the thinking of later social and political theoreticians of consequence.

A second optimistic rebel, François M. C. Fourier (1772–1837), proposed to eliminate the evils flowing from machinofacture and the unfairness of capitalism by converting the social order into a string of independent, essentially self-sufficient communities, called *phalanstères*. A federal union of communities would replace the traditional state.

Fond of mathematics, Fourier prepared his schemes with rigid exactness. Each community would embrace some four hundred families, dwelling in an apartment block equipped with nurseries, communal dining halls, and lecture rooms. Under attractive conditions members would work on the land and in mills, producing practically all the necessities of existence. To avoid the monotony of routine, men and women would switch from job to job; plenty of serene leisure would be available to profit from the higher values of life.

As with other Utopian socialists, Fourier reposed profound faith in the altruistic instincts of men. He believed, too, in the idea of progress and the perfectibility of man. In the fullness of time, millions of Homers, Molières, and Newtons would walk the earth! Rather pitifully in old age, he awaited a patron to provide funds for a pilot community in which happiness and prosperity would reign and start an experiment that would transform the world.

In point of fact, better than fifty Fourieristic colonies were established in Europe and the United States, some of which survived until after the First World War. Emerson described the short-lived community of intellectuals gathered at Brook Farm near Boston as "a perpetual picnic, a French Revolution in the small." Yet certain of the visions of Fourier found lodgment in the armory of later advocates of radical social and economic change.

The regime of Louis Philippe had no more relentless adversary than Étienne Cabet (1788–1856), theoretician of a full-bodied plan of communal living that captivated some underprivileged Parisians. A revolutionary republican in outlook, he was obliged for a time to go into exile in England. In *Voyage en Icaria,* Cabet argued that all property should be collectively owned, production should be minutely planned by servants of the state, and equality among citizens should extend even to the kind of clothes they wore. A company of his followers crossed the Atlantic in 1848, practicing what he preached in Texas and subsequently at Icaria, Illinois, which outlived the Fourier experiments.

More popular with hard-pressed wageworkers were the anticapitalist doctrines of youthful Louis Blanc (1811–1882), set out in vivid and persuasive language. Blanc represented a new image in the top echelons of

French social thought. His *L'Organisation du Travail (Organization of Labor)* contended that competition was the supreme enemy of the good society, and he believed that the system of capitalistic production was nearing its end. Equality in wages should be the norm; the government should establish cooperative workshops and collective farms, which would be owned by the workmen. Government, moreover, should guarantee employment to all able-bodied citizens. State officials, in other words, should plan the national economy so as to assure jobs for everyone.

No friend of King Louis Philippe—and also uncompromisingly hostile to Bonapartism—Blanc published a blistering indictment of the first decade of the July monarchy; extensively read, it helped to prepare minds for revolutionary violence, though the author personally declaimed against an appeal to force. Through his newspaper *Reform*, Blanc called incessantly for votes to all men as the indispensable preliminary to legislation to implement his program. Temporarily, during the upheaval of 1848, certain of his dreams were fulfilled and his writings exerted an enduring impact upon collectivist thought in France.

"Property is theft," proclaimed Pierre J. Proudhon (1809–1865) in his sensational *Qu'est-ce que le Propriété? (What is Property?)*. This radical heresy naturally attracted attention in Parisian circles concerned with social theories. A desperately sincere writer, a born polemicist endowed with an exceptionally keen brain, the picturesque style of Proudhon brought him as much publicity, perhaps, as his doctrine. Indeed, there is much that is enigmatic in his writings and tantalizingly inconsistent, so that, while he has been dubbed the "father of anarchism" and though he powerfully influenced the content of anarchist theory, he has also been identified as an intellectual herald of antidemocratic totalitarianism or fascism.

Private ownership of productive property Proudhon condemned on the reasoning that it yielded benefits to a privileged few out of the sweat of wageworkers. He wished a society in which economic equality existed, though he was not much interested in material things; "joyous poverty," he taught, would prevail in the perfect society. A deeply religious being, who traced many of his theories to the Scriptures, Proudhon was violently anticlerical. Above all, he thoroughly distrusted a powerful state, demanded, in fact, that it be swept away. Yet, like Louis Blanc, he opposed revolutionary action and advocated peaceful change.

The influence of Proudhon reached crescendo only after the Age of Metternich, and that was likewise true of the teachings of Karl Marx. Marx took up residence in Paris in the fermenting forties, which afforded him a splendid opportunity to study the varied assaults on capitalism in circulation there. His belief in the inevitable struggle between property owners and the propertyless, between the bourgeois class and the proletariat, and his belief in materialism, and even lesser tenets of his creed struck firmer root during his Paris days. And there too, Marx became acquainted with Friedrich Engels, destined to be his lifelong benefactor and collaborator. Together they agreed, "The philosophers have only interpreted the world in divers ways; the need, however, is to change it."

A New Revolution

In the late forties, France, in common with the rest of Europe, was tormented by a sharp recession in commerce and manufacturing and by a severe agricultural crisis. So great was unemployment that a third of Parisian households, it was estimated, depended upon charity to live. By means of public banquets, powerful currents of opinion were worked up against the July monarchy. After-dinner speakers smote king and counsellors hip and thigh, and their telling blows were reiterated in the press.

In February of 1848, the Guizot ministry prohibited

a monster antimonarchical banquet in Paris. That decision unloosed a volcano. The National Guard, republicans and democrats, and embittered wage earners indulged in mass street demonstrations, punctuated with stentorian demands for franchise reform, honesty in administration, and relief of social distress. Guizot resigned. But mob rioting and bloody encounters with royal troops persisted until King Louis Philippe abdicated, murmuring that it took a little time even for that. The July monarchy collapsed with a minimum of dignity and a minimum of tears. "Neither a principle nor a national glory . . . a utility, an expedient," said one carping critic in a farewell declaration. Straightaway, a hastily assembled ministry proclaimed that France had become a republic.

As plain Mr. Smith, the king passed over to England, dying like his predecessor and his successor in a strange land. To England, too, went Prince Clemens Metternich, for the Paris uproar wrought like an electric current upon the entire Continent up to the "iron curtain" of the empire of the tsars.

Summary

A mob rising in Paris in 1830 inspired revolutionary outbreaks at several spots to the east, and that sequence of events was repeated in much larger dimensions in 1848. In the interval, the forces desirous of change, whether governmental or national or social, gained fresh momentum. And yet it is easy to acquire a distorted impression of the strength of liberalism.

Pressures for parliamentary institutions responsive to manhood suffrage and for the whole panorama of civil liberties were most pervasive in the cities and towns of western Europe. These places possessed only middling significance in the heart of the Continent and merely trifling importance to the East. All across Europe, the institutions and rooted ways of traditionalism and conservatism predominated.

Clashing imperial interests in the Near East, considerations of the general European power balance, and passionate national prides kept foreign offices on edge. To the avoidance of an armed explosion, the fluctuating "Concert of Europe" contributed substantially.

Whereas the advent of the railway and the steamship marked the end of the beginning of the machine era in Britain, these novelties heralded the dawn of an industrial economy on the Continent. As mid-century approached, steampower had more than begun to effect a revolution in transportation by land and by water. The spread of factories, moreover, disturbed conventional methods of manufacturing and accelerated the growth of the middle classes and of the propertyless city-dwellers, or proletariat. In France, though scarcely elsewhere, the emergence of a sense of proletarian class consciousness could be detected.

Men of the middle classes, for the most part, carried the torch for broader freedoms and national independence. From their ranks, too, came evangelists of social reformation and specific blueprints for a radical reordering of society. Patterns for human progress flourished most luxuriantly in Paris, the heir of unique speculative and revolutionary traditions. Spokesmen of the rural masses in areas where serfdom still persisted demanded the abolition of that relic of medievalism. Contrary to the prophecies of facile social theorists, capitalistic enterprise stood actually on the threshold of a marvelous, unexampled upsurge.

Depressed business conditions in the late 1840's, together with subnormal crop yields, caused widespread unemployment and wretchedness, and aggravated social discontent. A local revolt in the Two Sicilies in 1848 preceded the overthrow of the French July monarchy. These developments ushered in *"Le printemps des peuples"*—"the springtime of peoples." Although often called a turning point in European affairs, the revolutionary years 1848–1849 produced only modest alterations.

C H A P T E R . . . 4

The Harvest of Culture

If one accepted the proposition of the English historian Edward A. Freeman that "history is past politics," he would be satisfied to dismiss the Age of Metternich with the subjects considered in the preceding chapters. But another, richer, and more nourishing approach to the past insists that history embraces all that man has thought and done. It remains then to look at aspects of cultural and intellectual affairs on the Continent which gave distinction to the era from 1814 to 1848.

The Catholic Church

During the post-Waterloo generation, Roman Catholicism experienced a remarkable renaissance. Skepticism in the eighteenth century had penetrated French lay and clerical circles alike, and during the tumultuous storms of the French Revolution the church had been deprived of property and privileges, and the pope and other churchmen subjected to degrading humiliations.

Yet religious fervor mounted as the drama of Napoleon entered its last act. His downfall stimulated widespread longing to return to "the good old days" and therewith a reawakening of concern for spiritual values. Men who regarded the struggle against the little Corsican as a crusade wished to pay honor to God for the ultimate victory. And for many men and women, wearied by prolonged warfare and political confusion, a warm, consoling, all-embracing faith appealed with special force. Besides, public leaders, aristocratic lords and ladies, and many middle-class folk rallied to Roman Catholicism as a bulwark of order and sound morals, an institution to counteract revolutionary sentiments.

Not long after the restoration of the pope in Rome in 1814, special treaties or concordats were negotiated by the Vatican with Catholic states, defining the rights of the church and her clergy. The powerful Society of Jesus, which had been dissolved by papal decree in 1773, was re-established, though in Austria Metternich restricted the society to the predominantly Polish-inhabited province of Galicia, and even there limitations were imposed upon Jesuit zeal.

Rapidly, Jesuit fathers regained their former ascendancy at the Vatican and vigorously opposed movements to create independent national churches. Supported by influential men of letters, the Jesuits succeeded in centralizing Catholic ecclesiastical authority in Rome. That principle, known as ultramontanism, enabled popes to exercise greater power in church affairs than their predecessors had commanded for generations. Jesuits founded new colleges to teach Catholic principles and resumed their globe-wide literary and missionary activities. A dozen other religious societies for men and women were organized, among them the French Congregation of the Sacred Heart of Jesus and the reformed Ursulines of Vienna, which educated daughters of well-to-do families. Other groups concentrated on educational and charitable work among the poor, the sick, and the elderly.

Another sign of the Catholic rejuvenation was the erection of many religious buildings—seminaries, chapels, and churches, such as the costly Notre Dame de Lorette and St. Vincent de Paul in Paris. And the task of converting inhabitants of Asia and Africa to the Christian faith was modestly advanced. An Association for the Propagation of the Faith, founded at French Lyons in 1822, effectively promoted foreign missions. Into India, the Orient, and Africa penetrated zealous evangelists, and martyrdoms were not uncommon. Missionary work in some undeveloped areas of the globe laid the foundations for leading European powers' later claims to colonies.

It was in France, above all, that the Catholic revival was fostered by a set of writers who fought rationalist thought and reaffirmed the faith and doctrines of the church. Traditionalist in outlook, these authors worked to unite the resources of altar and crown—the security of the first with the authority of the other—against innovations that were abroad in Europe. In these writers' thinking, conventional social institutions were the gift of God, and to challenge them was tantamount to sacrilege. The leading light of theological conservatism was the gifted and versatile François-René de Chateaubriand (1768–1848). In his *Génie du christianisme,* he militantly assailed rationalism and proclaimed that Catholicism, which had promoted civilization in the past, must be the sheet anchor of society in the future. Grudgingly, as free thinking lost popularity, France had come face to face with reality, he thought, "she has recognized that the Catholic religion is like an anchor which alone can quiet her restlessness." Not intellectually profound, but charming as literature, the writings of Chateaubriand appealed strongly to the disillusioned and the insecure in an age of anxiety.

Equally impressed by historical continuity and horrified by the excesses of the French Revolution, Comte Joseph de Maistre (1754–1821) contended that an autocratic government and an infallible church could alone save Europe from unmerited destruction. As the absolute head of the church, he explained in his most important book *Du Pape* of 1819, the pope towered over secular rulers in the temporal as well as in the religious sphere. Like some other thinkers then and later, de Maistre ascribed public ills and disorders to the Protestant rejection of the divinely ordained Papacy. Widely read at the time, his books were repeatedly republished and are still in print.

Another professional exponent of Catholicism, Louis de Bonald (1754–1840), penned coldly eloquent essays to prove that anarchy was the child of irreligion. Only unqualified obedience to papal authority, he taught, could conquer the forces of revolution and transform the evil nature of man.

Though the Breton priest Félicité R. de Lamennais (1782–1854) as a young man denounced toleration and staunchly defended the inherited faith and the authority of church tradition over reason, he later switched and advocated freedom and separation of church from state. Without wavering in his loyalty to the pope, he nonetheless argued that the church must come to terms with the new currents of the age and cooperate in the economic and social reordering of society. Author of several books, Lamennais also published a short-lived newspaper *L'Avenir* on whose masthead stood the watchword "God and Liberty." He set out his ideas in orderly form in his most respected book *Paroles d'un croyant (Sayings of a Believer)* of 1834.

Specifically, Lamennais called for freedom of learning and press, for manhood suffrage and genuine parliamentary government, for recognition of human equality and universal brotherhood, and for a church financially independent of the government. As an initiator of "liberal Catholicism," he had something to do with converting Victor Hugo and other educated men from agnosticism; his eloquent, fervently moral writings proved an inspiration to later Catholic social thought. But his views stirred up a hornet's nest and an-

tagonized powerful churchmen. Lamennais was condemned, though not formally excommunicated, by the
Vatican. "Experience has proved . . . ," declared the
papal pronouncement, "that states distinguished for
wealth, for power, for glory have perished from this
single evil, unrestrained freedom of thought, freedom
of speech, and the love of novelties. To this is related
that deadly freedom . . . the liberty of the press."

In harmony with the concern of Lamennais for the
welfare of ordinary Frenchmen, a Sorbonne professor
Antoine F. Ozanam (1813–1853) established the Society
of St. Vincent de Paul. Enrolling laymen only, this organization carried on social work among the poor, the
sick, and the jobless; the society spread wherever
Roman Catholicism was practiced.

From his pulpit in Notre Dame Cathedral and his
historical study, Comte Charles de Montalembert (1810–
1870) furthered the cause of theological conservatism.
"We are the sons of the Crusades," he kept saying, "and
we will never yield to the sons of Voltaire." Yet, in fact,
"the sons of Voltaire" increased steadily, as was suggested by the frequent republication of the writings of
that eighteenth-century agnostic. Among the well-
educated, the lure of Catholic traditionalism competed
with the appeal of skepticism, and the propertyless
wage earners of Paris continued to be the most free-
thinking working-class population of Europe.

In spite of the general resurgence of Catholic
strength, anticlericalism had by no means disappeared.
It cropped up within the Italian minority which strug-
gled for national unity in the face of papal opposition.
Frenchmen who deeply resented the power of the
church in secular affairs or who were free thinkers
played a prominent part in the July revolution of 1830.
During the reign of Louis Philippe, Catholicism was
denied recognition as the state religion, and its monopo-
listic control over learning was withdrawn. Catholic
gains among the comfortably fixed seem to have been
more than counterbalanced by losses among the prop-

ertyless city-dwellers. In Spain and Portugal, too, laws curtailing the scope of church activities were placed on the statute books. Controversies over mixed marriages, that is, unions between Catholics and Protestants, provoked endless troubles in central Europe.

Under official pressure about 2,000,000 Uniates, who accepted the spiritual headship of the pope, but shared certain liturgical customs with the Orthodox Eastern Church, were coerced into the Russian national church. Following the Polish insurrection of 1830, in which Catholic clergy had participated, Tsar Nicholas I laid restrictions upon Catholic bishops and seminaries, and threatened to confiscate church properties. To papal protestations, the emperor replied that he was not fighting religion but was bent on preventing a second rebellion; he made a pilgrimage to Rome to explain his policy. Persecution actually strengthened the hold of the traditional faith upon the Polish masses. Recurrent strife with secular authorities, moreover, did not arrest the internal revival of Catholicism.

Protestantism and Its Thinkers

The Continental versions of Protestantism commanded many fewer adherents than either Roman Catholicism or Eastern Orthodoxy. Followers of Martin Luther predominated in the Scandinavian north, in the German states other than Austria, and were also found in Alsace and among western Slavs. Most of the Swiss and the Dutch belonged to Reformed or Calvinist churches, which also counted important minorities in France and in Hungary; a German-speaking minority of Hungary worshipped in the Lutheran tradition, for the most part, as did the revolutionary chieftain, Louis Kossuth; and a small band of Unitarian rationalists lived in the eastern Hungarian countries.

The king of Prussia, a devoted Calvinist, ordered in 1817 that his church and the Lutheran should merge. A common body of doctrines was devised, though not

universally accepted. Dissident Lutherans who boldly
set up independent congregations were subjected to
governmental pressure which led some of them to seek
new freedoms in the United States. Even so, the United
Evangelical Church of Prussia made up the largest
Protestant body on the Continent.

Fresh vitality was infused into Lutheranism by a resurgence of fiercely antirational pietistic campaigns conducted by aristocratic laymen and directed at peasants
and town workers. Worship was conducted in homes,
emphasis was laid upon a mystical sense of union with
the Creator, and little or no attention was given to a
systematic scheme of thought. For their emotional effer-
vescence, lay leaders among pietists were tagged "Hur-
rah Christians."

Before the eighteen-thirties, French Protestantism
showed few signs of vigor, but then quickening influences flowed across from Switzerland and Great Britain.
Men of the Protestant minority often attained promi-
nence in French public life, the outstanding example
being Guizot. Until 1848 the creed of Calvin was the
state religion of the Netherlands, but in that year full
toleration was at last accorded. It was in the Age of
Metternich that Continental Protestantism first concerned itself with the conversion of non-Christians bow-
ing down to wood and stone "from Greeland's icy
mountain to India's coral strand."

Most vigorous of German theologians was Friedrich
D. F. Schleiermacher (1768–1834), esteemed by admirers
as the ablest thinker and writer in Protestant circles
since John Calvin himself. Once a rationalist in outlook, Schleiermacher moved to the opposite extreme in
repudiating reason as the way to religious truth. Every
man, he thought, was endowed with an innate sense of
dependence upon an absolute Being. It was the responsibility of religion to bring man into harmony with
the Infinite. Christianity achieved that goal more effectively than any rival faith, for at the heart of Christianity was Christ himself, the reconciliation of the
finite to the eternal.

Conceiving of theology as flexible, Schleiermacher contended that basic beliefs must undergo steady refinement in the light of broader Christian experience and of growing knowledge of the universe. That approach to theology attracted considerable support among systematic Christian thinkers. For a time his personal and literary charm won him a popularity in Germany matching that of Chateaubriand in France.

The leading German philosopher of the post-Waterloo era, George W. F. Hegel (1770–1831), likewise concluded that Christianity was the most perfect religious system. He taught, too, in his popular University of Berlin lecture hall, that the Prussian royal autocracy represented the ideal state, and that war was a logical necessity to test the stuff of which a country was really made. Hegel shaped a comprehensive and intellectually abstract body of thought resting on the conviction of evolutionary progress. According to his method of reasoning, called dialectic, thinking proceeded by comparison and contrast into a fresh synthesis of knowledge. Hegel believed that everything was interrelated in a dynamic whole, and that an overarching, eternal, and Absolute Spirit existed. By contrasting the Absolute with the finite, he emerged with the highest universal idea, God.

Very much a philosopher for philosophers, Hegel is credited with the observation that "Only one man has understood me—and he does not." In the long run, the dialectic scheme of reasoning which Hegel employed exerted a larger intellectual impact than the content of his thought, which at many points could not be reconciled with the evidence of history or with scientific findings.

Biblical Studies

Scholarly scrutiny of the literature of the Bible and of the origins and early expansion of Christianity, emanating from Germany, exerted in time a profound influence upon Christian thought. Although studies of this character had started before the nineteenth century, they were now substantially advanced with Tübingen University as the focal point of research and writing. The chief investigator, Ferdinand C. Baur (1792–1860), insisted that accurate interpretations of Christianity could be obtained only by critical examination of original sources of information. He concluded that the Gospel of Matthew was the oldest account of the career and teachings of Jesus, that the vital essence of the faith resided in the Sermon on the Mount, and that several of the books of the New Testament believed to have been written by Paul came in fact from another hand. His writings and provocative university lectures imparted a decided impetus to learned study of the heritage of Christianity.

Something of the fame of Baur derives from the reputation of his student David F. Strauss (1808–1874), who in 1835 published a highly controversial *Leben Jesu (Life of Jesus)*. He dismissed much of the content of the New Testament as unacceptable to the critically-minded historian. So slender was the evidence, Strauss argued, that no wholly satisfactory biography of the founder of Christianity could be composed. It is not surprising that his conclusions aroused a storm of protest, which prevented him from obtaining appointment to a university chair. Translated into English by the novelist George Eliot, *The Life of Jesus* opened a new chapter in the scholarly study of the New Testament. Subsequent researches forced modification or abandonment of many of the ideas of these erudite Biblical researchers in Germany.

Orthodox Eastern Christianity

Far the greater part of the inhabitants of Russia and of the Balkan Peninsula were adherents of the Orthodox Eastern Church. This branch of Christianity was noted at this time, as for centuries it had been noted, for rigid observance of church traditions and for unchanging theological convictions. Yet each nationality obtained the right to use its own language in Orthodox public worship, in such schools as existed, and in religious literature.

Since the time of the reforms carried through by Tsar Peter the Great, the Orthodox Church of Russia had been tightly bound to the state and thus it remained until the Bolshevik *coup d'état* in 1917. In the long run, the absorption of the church by the state proved injurious to both parties. In many areas of life, educated Russians felt their country was inferior to the West, yet churchmen were convinced that Holy Russia possessed the only pure and true version of Christianity.

Though skepticism and agnosticism had great strength among the Russian privileged classes, they nonetheless openly supported the state church as essential for social and political stability. Outwardly, at least, most of the Russian masses, illiterate and superstitious, subscribed to the national church.

Tsar Alexander I, who passed through a variety of theological experiences, incorporated his mystical idealism in the Holy Alliance (page 19); in a mood of tolerance he permitted the establishment of a Bible society to circulate the Scriptures, and granted sanctuary to Jesuit fathers until 1820 when they were expelled from the empire. Conservative forces gained the ascendancy in Orthodoxy after Nicholas I was installed as emperor. The "iron tsar" equated loyalty to the official church with loyalty to the throne. He considered the clergy, an aide tells us, as an army with a bishop in command of each diocese, "the priests as officers, while the people are the mass of soldiers."

During the reign of Nicholas I, a band of Slavophile intellectuals, who regarded the Orthodox Church as a vital feature of the national inheritance, proclaimed that Russia had a sacred mission to bring all mankind under the sway of this institution. A small knot of intellectual critics, on the other hand, shrilly attacked the national church as the defender of all that was out of joint in the empire of the tsars. Under state auspices, new monasteries were erected, especially for women, and missionaries pressed into Asia on the work of evangelization.

The tsardom contained a bewildering array of Christian sects, some of them having seceded from the state church, others having been influenced by German immigrants, still others emerging spontaneously from Russian religious experience. Best known of them perhaps were the Old Believers (*Raskolniki*), who professed to be more orthodox than the Orthodox in faith and practice, and the Spirit Wrestlers, or *Dukobors*, whose pacifism, communal manner of living, and social idiosyncrasies antagonized the public authorities. No matter how much they were persecuted, the sectarian millions flourished well into the twentieth century.

At the beginning of the nineteenth century most Balkan Christians lived under the jurisdiction of the patriarch in Constantinople. Though subject to the Ottoman sultan, this dignitary exercised effective authority over Balkan Orthodoxy in matters of administration no less than of belief and practices. His subordinates likewise dominated the intellectual sphere in the Balkans. Self-seeking Greeks had captured the patriarchate, and through it they appointed the ruling churchmen all across the peninsula. Orthodox prelates —Greek in tongue and heritage—fostered the use of their own language in Balkan churches and schools.[1] Outside of the Greek-speaking areas, parish priests and monks came from the local nationalities—Serbian, Bulgarian, Rumanian. Apart from their religious ministrations, the lower clergy were the custodians of their several national languages and cultures.

Growing trade encouraged the expansion of a business class among the Balkan nationalities, some of

[1] Though the Orthodox Eastern Church in the Balkan Peninsula is often spoken of as the Greek Church, confusion will be avoided if the term "Greek" is confined simply to the church in the Greek-speaking districts.

whose members were touched with western ideas of secularism and nationalism. This social category effectively challenged the lordship of the patriarchate and its bishops in one Balkan area after the other, and diverted the emphasis in schooling from religious to secular subjects. The famous Greek monastery on Mt. Athos conducted a school in which both classical and modern learning were supplied.

While the upper clergy in the Greek-peopled districts remained loyal to the sultan, many a simple Greek priest aligned himself in the national liberation movement of the 1820's. As a sequel to political independence, a separate Orthodox Church, independent of the patriarchate, was established in Greece in 1833, and a good deal of monastic property was seized by the royal government.

Chafing under the authority of Greek-speaking prelates, Serb and Bulgar intellectuals and bourgeoisie demanded hierarchies of their own nationality. Autonomy was conferred upon the church in Serbia in 1832, but the Bulgars and the Rumanians had to wait two generations longer for their church to escape control by Greeks. By and large, Balkan churchmen devoted themselves quite as fully to promoting the political ambitions of their respective nationalities as to serving the interests of Christianity. Church and nationalism were inextricably intertwined.

The State of Jewry

The emancipation of Jewry in western and central Europe was linked up with the French revolutionary principles of freedom and equality. Though Napoleon had granted Judaism legal status in 1808, after his downfall restrictions upon Jewry reappeared. Jews suffered discriminatory treatment in Austria, where they were forbidden to own landed property or to enter government service or many of the professions; only legally authorized Jews might live in Vienna and carry on business transactions. Conditions were much the same in the Italian states, and the ghetto was revived in Rome. Families of Jewish tradition were expelled from German commercial centers; in Frankfurt, the home of the affluent Rothschild bankers, Jews were confined to a restricted quarter until 1824. After 1830, invidious regulations against the Jews of Prussia were revoked piecemeal, and Jews gradually obtained civil and religious equality.

A fraction of German Jewry discarded parts of the traditional observance of the faith; in 1818 a "reformed" temple was organized in Hamburg, which was imitated by a few congregations in western Europe and in the United States. Assimilation of Jewry to the rest of the German community proceeded steadily; certain Jews, the father of Karl Marx for example, embraced the Christian religion.

Most Jews, however, clung tenaciously to ancient beliefs and time-honored ritualistic devotions. The main body of Jewry lived in the empire of the tsar, largely isolated from other Russian nationals. By and large, Jewish residence was confined to a western zone of the empire, the Pale of Settlement. There the Jews preserved their special customs and costumes, their Yiddish language and schools, along with their religious heritage. Subjected to civil and social disabilities, the east European Jews were victims of personal indignities and sometimes of shameful mob violence.

European Literature

In the forepart of the nineteenth century, men of letters displayed an unusual flair for major contributions in more than one variety of literature. It is common to refer to this period as the romantic era.

Romanticism, which permeated so much of the life of the mind and the spirit, represented a self-conscious reaction to the stiff formalism of the eighteenth century. Starting with poetry, the romantic approach spread to fiction, to drama, and to the writing of history. Instead of the rational in human nature, writers chose to allow free play to the imagination. Emotional individualism, subjectivity, and ideals of freedom crowded aside the severely intellectual and oftentimes artificial. "Romanticism," cried the Frenchman Victor Hugo, "is liberalism in literature."

Romantic literature derived its temper and sought themes in the legendary and the picturesque of the Middle Ages or in exotic tales of the East, Greece especially. Writers interpreted the chivalric epoch of medieval Europe in brilliant colors, overlooking its narrowness and crudities. By the end of the Age of Metternich, romanticism as the dominant accent in literature had practically spent itself.

For the Continent, the principal inspiration to the romantic mood came from the writings of Jean Jacques Rousseau (1712–1778), which had wide circulation in France after Waterloo. It was Chateaubriand, above all, who gave a patent of respectability to French romantic literature. The first section of *Les Martyrs*, asserting the superiority of Christianity, ranks among the most faultless pieces of imaginative writing in the French language. Chateaubriand's fluency and colorful style, his addiction to the emotional in human nature, fostered the cult of romanticism and encouraged a spate of lyric poetry.

Romanticist Poetry

Poetic expression was rich in imagery and reflected thoroughly individualistic talents, so well exhibited in the verse of Alphonse de Lamartine (1790–1869). Once noted for dignified elegies and melodious tributes to the love of nature or to God (*Méditations Poétiques*), Lamartine later attempted—as in the admirable *Jocelyn* —to recall historical periods and to portray the soul of a lonely man in the search for perfection. Stoical despair gripped Alfred de Vigny in *Moïse,* prized as one of the most impressive pieces of French poetry.

The peer of these poets in style, and doubtless their

master in color and diction, was the most famous European author of his time, Victor Hugo (1802–1885). His poetry possessed an encyclopedic quality—classical odes, paeans to the Greeks struggling for independence (*Les Orientales*), glorifications of Napoleon and of France, or romantic evocations of nature. Intensely amorous, Alfred de Musset (1810–1857) sang of tragic love affairs with a sensitivity and a passionate sincerity that captivated the young in years and in spirit (*Les Nuits*). Regarded by some authorities as the most authentically French of modern poets, de Musset allowed his fertile imagination to run fast and free.

German romantic poetry had profound expression in the *Faust* of Johann W. von Goethe (1749–1832), put in final form only a year before his death. For this immortal work, the most celebrated of all German imaginative writers drew upon his immense knowledge of mythology, folklore, and natural science. Goethe exerted no inconsiderable influence upon poems of love and melancholy composed by Heinrich Heine (1797–1856), perhaps the most popular, as surely the most versatile, of German lyricists. As shown in his best-loved production, *Die Nordsee,* Heine excelled in brilliance of imagery and in language of simple but compelling force. Several of Heine's ballads (*Die Lorelei,* for example) achieved enduring, international appreciation. As a member of a Young Germany literary movement, Heine advocated civil liberties, popular government, and a moderate sort of German nationalism, though his happiest years were lived in Paris. In the romantic era, too, the anthems of the German nation, *Die Wacht am Rhein* (1840) and *Deutschland, Deutschland über alles,* were first composed and sung.

In *Spaziergänge eines Wiener Poeten (Walks of a Vienna Poet)* the aristocratic Anastasius Grün (Count Anton A. Auersperg, 1808–1876), expressed faith in parliamentary government and flailed away at the repressive literary censorship. Not a poet of the first order of ability by any stretch of the imagination, Grün nevertheless attracted attention by the vigor of his appeals for freedom. Scornful of Prince Metternich, he wrote defiantly,

"Austria is it, honest, open, on her best behavior,
   See, she asks, may I make so free as to be free?"

Like the writings of other Austrians critical of the prevailing political and social structure, his verse was often printed in Germany and smuggled into Vienna.

Distinguished for the high quality of his poetry, not its quantity, the foremost Italian lyricist, Alessandro Manzoni (1785–1873) voiced a desire for national unity and stirred readers out of political lethargy. A moving ode on the death of Napoleon, *Il Cinque Maggio (Fifth of May)* is treasured as the noblest production of its kind in Italian literature. Also calculated to arouse national emotions were patriotic odes by Giacomo Leopardi (1798–1837), some of them—to Italy and to Dante —banned by the Austrian censorship as dangerously subversive.

Slavic Literature

Until the nineteenth century, little writing in Slavic tongues attained international acceptance, for one reason because not much other than religious literature was written. Indeed, several Slav vernaculars—Serbo-Croat, Slovene, and Slovak, for example—were only now established as literary languages with grammars and dictionaries. This important task was carried out by dedicated Slav linguists who believed the conversion of peasant dialects into a form suitable for literature was indispensable for the cultural progress of their nationality.

Much was accomplished in the reduction of the Russian language to rules by Alexander S. Pushkin (1799–1837). The "prodigious Pushkin," as his countrymen called him, ushered in the golden age of Russian literature. Though of aristocratic birth, he belonged in spirit to the emerging Russian intelligentsia, defined as "those who think and talk and write of change." His poetry on the theme of freedom and *Lines sent to Siberia*, lauding the exiled Decembrist rebels, won him favor in both imperial and Communist Russia. His best production, *Eugene Oneygin*, a national epic ending in a melancholic vein, has had an enduring impact upon Russian authors. It described the easy-going way of life of the aristocratic caste and vividly recounted popular folk tales. Pushkin was influenced by the English lyricist Lord Byron, as was Mikhail I. Lermontov (1814–1841), a turbulent Russian personality whose romantic verse unloosed sharp arrows at the sordid and the detestable in the empire of the tsars. With uncanny precision Lermontov in the *Prophecy* forecast the coming of the Bolshevik hurricane.

Adam Mickiewicz (1798–1855) lives on as the greatest national poet of the Poles, the teacher and political prophet of his own people and of other subjugated nations struggling for independence and social fairness. Some experts consider him the best of Slav poets, superior even to Pushkin. His moving epic *Pan Tadeuz (Sir Thaddeus)* is replete with romantic descriptions of Polish country living and rural beauty, and with portraits of typical Polish aristocrats. Ardent patriotism and genial humor blend with poignant lamentations over the bitter sufferings of his beloved Poland, crushed into submission after the 1830 rebellion.

As an example of sentimental and romantic poetry of the smaller Slav nationalities may be cited the intensely patriotic *Slavy Dcera (Daughter of Slava)* by Jan Kollár (1793–1852). A long series of sonnets, it fiercely attacked German dominance over Slavs, championed Slav national interests, and proclaimed a better and brighter future for Slavs everywhere.

Romantic Drama

French playwrights clearly held first place in productions for the theater. *Henri III et sa Cour* by Alexander

Dumas, the elder (1803–1870), is regarded as the first successful play of the romanticist type. In other highly imaginative dramas he exalted human passion and rebellion against established social conventions, such as in *Anthony*. The presentation of Hugo's *Hernani* of 1830 in verse form provoked a wild outburst in Paris, but signalized at once the victory and the impending decline of romantic drama. Light comedy came into its own with the creations of Eugène Scribe (1791–1861), which poked fun at the narrow interests and moral standards of the upthrusting French bourgeoisie; catchy songs, frothy humor, and allusions to current events captivated Parisian theatergoers.

Among dramatists writing in German, the commanding personality was the Viennese Franz Grillparzer (1791–1872). In plays based upon Austrian history, such as *Ein treuer Diener (A Faithful Servant)*, he was minded to teach loyalty to the ruling house, yet censorship arbitrarily banned plays that were critical of the prevailing order, and they had to be filed away for performance at some time in the future. His most prized drama, *Des Meeres und der Liebe Wellen (The Waves of the Sea and of Love)*, a dramatic love tragedy founded upon ancient legends, failed at first to capture public favor, but in time it became standard fare on the German-speaking stage.

The best loved comedy of tsarist Russia was, doubtless, Nikolai Gogol's (1809–1852) *Government Inspector*, a rollicking tale of provincial officials, their lackadaisical performance of duties, their obsequiousness. Stinging ridicule and revelations of the growing authority of money in Russian society feature in the play.

Novels of the Romantic Era

Easily, the novel held first place in the writing of the time, especially popular being the productions combining ascertained historical fact with a large admixture of fiction. Continental authors took to heart the amazing success achieved by the *Waverly Novels* of Sir Walter Scott. Set in the Middle Ages *Notre Dame de Paris* by Hugo revived the mystical qualities of medieval living, its passions, strengths, and shortcomings, as suggested by the massive cathedral on the Seine. Typically romantic in imagination and opulent in literary style, the novel depicted Paris and Parisians as Hugo wished they had been rather than as they actually were. Collecting a band of collaborators, the elder Dumas poured out thrilling inventive tale after thrilling inventive tale—*Les Trois Mousquetaires* and *Le Comte de Monte-Cristo*. At the time of these books' appearance and ever since, Dumas has appealed to readers seeking exciting melodrama rather than penetrating analyses of human nature or historical realities.

The classical novel *I Promessi Sposi (The Bethrothed)* by the Italian Manzoni accurately recaptured the spirit and thought of Lombardy under Spanish rule. A seed-volume in the literary revival of the Italian nation, it was one of the most powerful of romantic creations, and politically very influential. In its final form, the novel was written in the Tuscan dialect, thereafter the tongue for the finest Italian prose productions. That trail blazer of imaginative Russian prose, Gogol, in *Taras Bulba* beautifully and colorfully depicted the heartaches and joys of a sixteenth-century Cossack household in his native Ukraine. It is replete with stirring adventure, warfare, and warm love of country.

Romances of mystery took their place alongside the historical novel. *Peter Schlemihl* by the German Adelbert von Chamisso (1781–1838), telling of a poor fellow who sold his soul to the devil for a large fortune, achieved an international reputation. Poetic and charming were the creations of the Dane, Hans Christian Andersen (1805–1875). His extensively translated *Fairy Tales* delighted by their tender emotion and feeling for the mysterious elements of nature.

The virtues and vices of the peasantry found an engaging expositor in George Sand (1804–1876), pen name of Baronne Dudevant. A lady tending to be rebellious in her thought, a lady of advanced views, she composed novels (*Indiana*) quarreling with prevailing social mores and then turned to idealizations of French rustics and their way of life (*François de Champi*). For rural Germany, Theodor Storm (1817–1888) in *Immensee* focused upon an old gentleman who reminisced about the love escapades of his youth. The abuses of serfdom, the profligacy of the landlords, the upthrusting tradesmen of Russia were vividly painted—and with rollicking wit and humor—by Gogol in *Dead Souls*. It encouraged agitation, that bore fruit in the next generation, to wipe out the iniquity of serfdom.

Two outstanding French storytellers defy classification in any general grouping: Henri Beyle (1783–1842), known by the pseudonym of Stendhal, and Honoré de Balzac (1799–1850). Stendhal, for his aversion to conventions and his preoccupation with the hidden springs of human conduct, is pointed to as a pathfinder for the realistic novelists later in the nineteenth century. His approach exerted a lasting influence upon writers of novels who meticulously studied his creations, such as *Le Rouge et le Noir*. This work recalls the changing social atmosphere in France after Waterloo. Instead of seeking a career in the army, a rather bizarre bourgeois youth choses the black garb of the churchman and tries to kill his former mistress for which he is himself put to death.

More sharply than Stendhal, Balzac cut loose from the romanticist mood and realistically—and elaborately —described what he had personally observed in the French bourgeois society of his generation. His *Comédie Humaine*, which started to appear in 1829, ran into ninety-seven volumes illuminating provincial and Parisian life, political and philosophical interests, military and social affairs—in short, a vast, photographically faithful panorama of a highly important segment of

European mankind. If he had written nothing other than *Eugénie Grandet,* Balzac would have assured himself of a secure place in the history of French letters.

The Loom of History

In the course of the Age of Metternich, even as the art of the novel moved from flowery romanticism in the direction of realism, so the writing of history shifted from an "artistic" approach to the past toward dispassionate narrative. Particularly Frenchmen, in the romantic heyday, composed picturesque and diverting histories or works reflecting their own political convictions or philosophical outlook. Highly imaginative and eloquent, Jules Michelet (1798–1874) crowded his pages with fervent love of France and affection for the common man. His multi-volumed *Histoire de France* resembles a set of tableaux, instead of an orderly reconstruction of events; as he candidly acknowledged, the treatment of the Middle Ages, featured by a dazzling portrait of Joan of Arc, possessed distinctively imaginative qualities. Rather in the same mold is his brilliant, though factually inaccurate, history of the great French Revolution. A spirited apologia for that epochal event, the *Histoire de la Revolution* conveys the humanitarianism of Michelet, his consuming patriotism, and an artistic charm. Read as literature rather than to learn what actually happened, Michelet is still rewarding.

Seeking to explain the past after the manner of science, François-Pierre Guizot, university professor as well as statesman, composed a *Historie Générale de la Civilisation en Europe* and an *Essai sur l'Histoire de France*. While the first is a useful philosophical survey of European civilization, the second is a pioneer adventure in treating the unfolding of a society in the spirit of objective science; these works served as textbooks in colleges on both sides of the Atlantic. In the thinking of Guizot, the past had evolved in a logical manner, and civilization was identical with progress.

As he read the past—and peered into the future—Guizot decided that the middle classes constituted the strong and significant elements in any society; just about this time, Karl Marx was reaching the conclusion that the bourgeoisie had fulfilled its historical mission and was doomed to extinction.

Guizot's arch rival in public affairs, Adolphe Thiers, made a reputation as a writer on French history from the eve of the great Revolution to the death of Napoleon. His most valuable work was a massive *Histoire du Consulat et d'Empire,* admirably written, but often degenerating into little more than a glowing eulogy of Bonaparte. It imparted an impetus to the growth of the Napoleonic legend. It lacks, however, the literary grace of Michelet and the speculative appeal of Guizot, for imagination and schematic theorizing had no place in Thiers' conception of the responsibility of the historian.

Attuned to the dominant temper of the age was a *History of the Russian State* in a dozen stately volumes, prepared by Nicholas Karamzin (1766–1826), court historian and counselor of Tsar Alexander I. Intensely laudatory and fervently patriotic, this work pictured Mother Russia as surpassing imperial Rome in her finest decades. "It is said," wrote Karamzin, "that our history is less interesting than others . . . I do not think so. We had our Charlemagne—Vladimir; our Louis XI —Tsar Ivan; our Cromwell—Godunov, and, in addition, a sovereign unlike any other . . . Peter the Great. . . ." Karamzin praised the Russian autocratic regime, painted the Orthodox Church as spotless and without blemish, defended the institution of serfdom, and predicted that the magnificent past of Russia assured a resplendent future provided the gentry—Karamzin's own social caste—cooperated harmoniously with the tsar. As well as giving form and substance to a Russian version of philosophical conservatism, Karamzin established Russian prose as a literary art, and provided an enormous historical quarry from which men of letters later dug out themes.

Distinguished practitioners of romantic history for other Slavs were the Czech František Palacký (1798–1876), and Joachim Lelewel (1786–1861), author of a dramatically colored history of the Poles. Political leader and historian alike, Palacký in his nationalistic *History of Bohemia* idealized the medieval greatness of his Czech countrymen and their heroic struggles with German neighbors and rivals. Designed not only to recall the past, but to kindle enthusiasm for the national future, this history, like similar writings by other historians of subject nationalities, reached its objectives. The writing and reading of history were intimately bound up with the awakening of national consciousness.

In the meantime, fresh winds concerning the nature of historical scholarship had started to blow from great German shrines of learning and research. Pre-eminent was the Berlin master Leopold von Ranke (1795–1886), who wished to reconstruct the past as it "actually occurred," in his own phrase. To that end, he insisted upon critical study of original manuscripts and papers in contrast to the free-wheeling impressionism of the romanticist school. He led the way, too, in detailed analyses of the principal authors upon whom he relied in his works.

For all his profession of objectivity, von Ranke did not entirely escape the force of his personal convictions, though he was much more impartial than many of his successors. His learned *Die römischen Päpste (History of the Popes)* dispassionately recounted the stormy epoch of the Reformation and remains a classic of historical investigation and writing. After composing many other books of distinction, he commenced a universal history extending from ancient Egypt onward. By the time of his death at the age of ninety, he had completed seven volumes, reaching deep into medieval Europe. Regarded by many historians as the ideal member of their craft, the influence of von Ranke upon his profession has been widespread and enduring.

Romanticism in the Fine Arts

Concerning the role of Frenchmen as painters in the nineteenth century, the director of the Berlin art gallery, von Tschudi, wrote, "France was like Italy in the Renaissance, and Holland in the seventeenth century, the classic land of painting." Paris resembled a battleground on which artists who preferred classical traditions contended with romanticists bent upon freedom of expression, faithful imitation of nature, action, and color. Instead of the mythology of classical Greece and Rome, romanticist artists sought subject matter from the Middle Ages or the Orient, from contemporary events or the quiet countryside—all of which the classicists disdained.

"Drawing is everything; color is nothing," summed up the creed of Jean A. Ingres (1780–1867), prince of the Parisian classical group. The "Voeu de Louis XIII" ("The Vow of Louis XIII") demonstrated Ingres' allegiance to line and linear design and his distaste for color. Ingres' strong-willed personality inspirited like-minded painters, exerted a considerable impact upon French art, and manfully though vainly resisted "the invasion of the Barbarians," as he tagged romanticists.

In the vanguard of the opposing camp stood Jean L. Géricault (1791–1824), who strove to translate his devotion to liberty onto canvas. The wrecking of the ship "Medusa" and the escape of a few of the crew on a raft furnished the inspiration for his important "Radeau de Méduse" ("Raft of the Medusa"). He questioned the survivors of the tragedy, studied suffering in a hospital —both novel activities for painters—and then produced a gigantic picture of the wretched sailors crouching on their frail raft. The minute detail, the anguish of the victims, and the pathos of the episode foreshadowed the standard interests of romanticism in painting. Ridiculed by classicists, Géricault nonetheless won a brilliant disciple in the person of Eugène Delacroix (1798–1863).

Called the finest intellect of the French romanticists, Delacroix stressed brilliant coloring and lavish portrayal of human emotions as in the "Massacre de Scio," which caused critics to bewail "the massacre of painting." From this imaginative re-creation of an atrocity in the Greek struggle for independence, Delacroix moved on to scenes of Oriental life and decorative projects for public buildings. For opulence of color and magnificent scenery, "L'Entrée des Croisés à Constantinople" ("The Entry of the Crusaders into Constantinople") belongs in a class apart. Mounted Crusaders advance with waving banners amidst bloodshed, pillage, and natives begging for mercy. Constantinople forms the background with smoke pouring from dwellings and ships and threatening skies overhead. Color masses possess an unusual density, and lights and darks are skillfully contrasted in a manner characteristic of romanticist creations.

With Géricault leading the way, a set of French artists revived landscape painting. Lovers of nature established themselves near the village of Barbizon and painted in the open—something previously unheard of. Camille Corot (1796–1875) wonderfully exploited the picturesque beauties of rural France and her peasants, while Théodore Rousseau (1812–1867) excelled in precise, elegant reproductions of trees, terrain, and other features of the countryside. The art of political and social caricature was raised to new levels by Honoré Daumier (1808–1879). In Parisian humorous journals, he heaped caustic ridicule upon the bustling, uncouth middle-class society of finance and commerce. Worshiper of Napoleon that he was, he satirically lampooned "bourgeois" King Louis Philippe, and, when one of his caricatures transgressed the canons of good taste, Daumier was tossed into jail.

French art rather cast the productions of painters of other Continental countries into the shade. German artists, it is true, prepared huge allegories on the history of their country and in so doing revived the art of mural decoration. Their leader, Peter von Cornelius (1783–1867), had an unusual knack for conceiving vast pictorial designs, though he had less technical skill in executing them. Under the sway of German emphases, Poles and Czechs also painted large historical works calculated to arouse patriotic sentiments among their co-nationals. At Vienna, Ferdinand G. Waldmüller (1793–1865) earned lasting renown for portraits of prominent worthies, Beethoven among them, and for landscapes. The most important Russian painting, "The Appearance of Christ to the People," a colossal tableau of great vitality by Alexander Ivanov (1806–1858), occupied almost the entire creative career of the artist. It laid the foundations of national painting in the empire of the tsars, separate from the fashions current in the west of Europe.

French sculptors, no less than French painters, turned out the most notable works of the early nineteenth century. On the whole, they broke away from the flabby mannerisms of the previous century. A classicist François J. Bosio (1769–1845) carved a superb equestrian statue of Louis XIV, and his co-worker Jean P. Cortot produced the "Apothéose de Napoleon" for the Arc de Triomphe in Paris, classical in conception though theatrical in gestures. For that renowned monument, François Rude (1784–1855) mingled classical traditions with romanticist novelties in an exciting composition of men going off to the revolutionary wars—"Le Départ des Volontaires de 1792." Roman costumes adorned fighters whose expression of emotional patriotism is purely in the romantic vein. On the Place de la Concorde in the heart of Paris stand pert female representations of the cities of Lille and Strasbourg done by James Pradier (1792–1852), whose busy chisel was also responsible for a dozen chaste sentinels surrounding the tomb of Napoleon in Les Invalides.

King Ludwig I of Bavaria dreamed of converting his capital of Munich into a new Athens. To fulfill the plans, sculptors set about carving busts of eminent

Germans of the past; the best of the workers, Ludwig von Schwanthaler (1802–1848), infused romantic simplicity into his statues, among them a soaring bronze "Bavaria." For Berlin, Christian Rauch (1777–1857) created a lively and dignified statue of Frederick the Great on horseback; at the base were the principal colleagues of the king in advancing Prussia to a place among the great powers. A realistic and stylistically vigorous Dresden sculptor, Ernst F. Rietschel (1804–1861), embodied notable memorials in stone to Goethe and Schiller in his home city and in Weimar, and to Luther in Worms.

Among Italians, the leading light in the visual arts was the sculptor Antonio Canova (1757–1822), more highly regarded by enthusiastic contemporaries than by posterity. Of his many productions, "Love and Psyche Watching a Butterfly" which is moderately classical in design, and a splendid cenotaph of Maria Christina who was the daughter of Austrian Empress Maria Theresa, have most effectively withstood the test of time. The latter, installed in a Vienna church, consists of a tall, graceful marble pyramid, with mourning figures in procession to the open door of the tomb, before which waits a youthful spirit of death. Under the sway of classical Greece, the Danish sculptor Bertel Thorwaldsen (1770–1844) carved scores of pieces, the most refined of which led critics to speak of him as a sort of second Phidias. His beloved *Lion of Lucerne* dramatized the heroism of the Swiss guard which was butchered in 1792 while trying to protect ill-starred Louis XVI of France. With the passing of time, the sculptures of Thorwaldsen, which were not in fact the creations of another Phidias, came to possess little more than historical significance.

Architecture

The decades from Waterloo to the revolutionary explosions of 1848 witnessed a wonderful outburst of building in Continental cities, capitals especially, from Paris to St. Petersburg (Leningrad). Architects designed all manner of public structures—museums and art galleries, libraries and theaters, government buildings and prisons, markets and even railway stations late in the forties. A few noteworthy churches were erected or radically reconstructed, though not many palatial residences of distinction appeared.

French leadership in architectural achievements yielded to German. In Berlin and its environs, the Prussian state architect Karl F. von Schinkel (1781–1841) built several great structures, mostly in the spirit of Greek revivalism. His finest, most sensitive creation, the Altes Museum, served as a gallery for Greek and Roman art works. He also drew the plans for a mediocre cathedral in the Prussian capital, a theater, a fine memorial to the dead of the Napoleonic wars, and an arsenal. With King Frederick William IV, who prided himself on his talent as an architect, providing the designs, von Schinkel erected religious and secular buildings in neighboring Potsdam.

The lofty cultural ambitions of King Ludwig I converted Bavarian Munich into a community of beautiful buildings and the leading art center of the Germanies. Patterns from classical antiquity jostled with neo-Renaissance styles. The royal architect Franz K. L. von Klenze (1784–1864), who had been trained in the classical traditions of France, opened his career with a modest gallery for sculptures and followed along with a mixture of Greek, Roman, and Renaissance styles in the famous Glypothek and Old Pinakothek museums in which paintings, sculptures, and archaeological treasures were displayed.

Von Klenze and lesser architects also adorned Munich with a court church in Byzantine-Renaissance style, a new Pinakothek art gallery, a national theater and library, a hall of heroes, and a splendid university. During the Second World War many of these buildings were severely damaged, but they have been restored. By 1848, when Ludwig I was forced to abdicate, whole squares in Munich and entire sections of streets had been handsomely transformed, and the city had advanced to front rank in German art and beauty.

For admirers of Gothic architecture, it was cheering to learn in 1842 that plans to finish the Cologne Cathedral, which had been laid away during the Reformation, had been revived. Fully completed only in 1880, this majestic edifice conformed faithfully to the Gothic style at its purest. Major building projects were likewise executed in Karlsruhe, Dresden, Breslau (Wroclau after 1945), the chief cities of Baden, Saxony, and Prussian Silesia, respectively, and in the port community of Hamburg. Vienna lagged well behind other German-speaking municipalities; her great age of construction would come in the second half of the century.

Many grandiose architectural plans of Napoleon in Paris were left uncompleted when he passed from the stage. Several of them were finished during the reign of Louis Philippe—for instance, the Madeleine church in Paris, the crowning glory of the Roman revival. The noblest memorial to Bonaparte, the massive Arc de Triomphe, was likewise completed and, as previously mentioned, lavishly embellished with sculptures.

Whereas before 1800, great structures in St. Petersburg were the products of Italian architectural genius or an occasional Frenchman or Scotchman, in the era of Alexander I and Nicholas I, native architects, such as Karl I. Rossi (1775–1849), were more commonly employed. Classical Roman models supplied the inspiration for several magnificent structures in the Russian capital, the pride and joy of Tsar Peter I and scarcely a century old. A Stock Exchange, an Admiralty, a theater, and a senate house rose there in rapid order, as well as Kazan Cathedral, an immense pile suggestive of St. Peter's in Rome, converted by the Communists into a much-frequented antireligious museum. The German von Klenze had charge of designing the well-known Hermitage museum and art gallery, which hints at Greek revivalism. Forty years in the building was the neo-classical St. Isaac's Cathedral, the creation of a French architect August R. de Montferrand (1786–1858), who had helped to construct the Madeleine. Possibly the finest piece of architecture of the era, St. Isaac's is noted for its magnificent marbles and granite columns and for a great dome framed in iron.

Music

The romantic mood attained its fullest and most perfect flowering in the realm of music, the international "language of the emotions." Distaste for classical patterns, emphasis on individualism and innovation, and fondness for vivid coloring distinguished musical compositions as with romanticism in other areas of the mind and spirit. Like men of letters, the finest composers excelled in versatility. Musical culture profited, moreover, by the appearance of instruments that were more accurate mechanically; the manufacture of better qualities of iron and steel, for instance, made possible the creation of more perfect pianos. The foundation of societies to cultivate appreciation of music and of new schools to teach music testified to the growing popularity of musical art. Patronage for artists and performances came increasingly from aspiring middle-class families, instead of the aristocracy and church as in the past.

Late in the eighteenth century, the standing of Vienna as the special home of musical artistry had been firmly established by Josef Haydn (d. 1809) and Wolfgang A. Mozart, who put the finishing touches on the most thrilling of operas, *Die Zauberflöte* (*The Magic Flute*), in 1791, the year of his death. Vienna's prestige was consolidated by the towering genius of Ludwig van Beethoven (1770–1827), who, like Prince Metternich, drifted to the "Queen City" on the Danube from the Rhineland. His numerous and diversified compositions represented a bridge, as it were, between classical formalism and the vogue of self-expression typifying romanticism. The stirring opera *Fidelio* by Beethoven, his nine great symphonies, his two masses, and his concertos and sonatas exhibit the abundant talent of the man at his finest. He wrote a large body of instrumental music—solos, trios, and quartets—distinguished, like his other compositions, by technical perfection, vitality of spirit, and rare nobility of feeling. By the tests of influence upon other composers and of sustained popularity, Beethoven belongs in the small elite of immortal musicians. To foster elegance in music the Vienna *Gesellschaft der Musikfreunde (Society of the Friends of Music)* was founded in 1812, and in 1841 the Vienna Philharmonic orchestra started on its wonderful career.

It has been written of Franz Schubert (1797–1828) that he "left the richest legacy of joy ever bequeathed to the world of music." Lyric songs by this precocious and short-lived son of Vienna, which he tossed off as easily as letters, possessed spontaneity, unusual exuberance, and much dreamy sentimentality. His melodies expressed a secular gaiety that was imagined to be distinctively Viennese. Though the classical composers of Vienna had cultivated dance music to a limited extent, it was in the Age of Metternich, known in Austria as the "Biedermeier" (Philistine) period, that this musical form acquired a reputation as art.

Two spirited composers, Josef Lanner (1801–1843) and his better-known contemporary, Johann Strauss the elder (1804–1849), enlivened Vienna with intoxicating dance rhythms. The waltzes of Strauss, a visitor commented, "stir the blood like the bite of a tarantula" —which must have been extremely stirring. Merry operettas replete with dance melodies had already appeared, but that musical diversion awaited fulfillment by the younger Johann Strauss (d. 1899) in the latter half of the century.

A passionate German patriot, Carl Maria von Weber (1786–1826), stimulated enthusiasm for national unity through songs for soldiers fighting Napoleon and in *Der Freischütz,* a dream-like opera. For that production, von Weber drew extensively upon old folk ballads and colorful legends of the forest, heralding the triumph of the romantic temper in opera. Nearly every category of formal music was cultivated by the fertile talent of Robert A. Schumann (1810–1856). He infused personal experiences into charming pieces for the piano or lilting melodies to accompany the poetry of Heinrich Heine.

Basic innovations in the character of operatic composition were introduced by the first creations of the tempestuous Richard Wagner (1813–1883), a careful student of Beethoven's music and his lifelong admirer. At · Dresden in 1843 he produced *Der fliegende Höllander* (*The Flying Dutchman*), inspired by a sailor's legend which Heine had put into German. Not less extravagantly romantic was *Tannhäuser* (1845), based upon old German myths collected by the Grimm brothers. It was remarkable for its orchestration and was staged with lavish pageantry. These productions have never ceased to thrill operagoers who have a taste for the Wagnerian approach.

Opera in the romantic vein enlisted several Italian musicians such as Gioachino Rossini (1792–1868). Charged with plagiarizing the techniques of other masters, Rossini wrote in a manner to appeal to middle-class appetites. A certain superficiality as well as a certain passion for republicanism characterize his most-prized production, *Guillaume* (*William*) *Tell.* The early operas of Giuseppe Verdi (1813–1901), dramatic and richly melodic, are indebted to the general mood of romanticism, the enchanting *Rigoletto* having its source in a drama by Victor Hugo.

French composers delighted in *opéra comique* noted for diverting instrumentation and topical text, which commented on contemporary customs, bourgeois tastes, and political aspirations. *La Muette de Portici* by Daniel F. Auber (1782–1871), the most reputable of his class, helped to touch off the Belgian revolt of 1830. Catering to middle-class audiences, the German-born Giacomo Meyerbeer (1791–1863), a disciple of Rossini, matched in opera the colorful emotionalism and the partiality for historical and legendary themes of the Parisian stage (*Les Hugenots*).

The bizarre, the iconoclastic, gorgeous coloring, and unconventional use of instruments figure prominently in the music of Hector Berlioz (1803–1869), who loved to dazzle, even to frighten audiences. Romanticism in French music reached a peak with the *Symphonie fantastique*, which earned Berlioz a place alongside of Hugo in literature and Delacroix in the fine arts.

Parisian partisans of the romantic style welcomed to their midst the Polish-born Frédéric F. Chopin (1810–1849). Writing only for the piano, on which he was himself a superb performer, Chopin produced elegant and emotionally exciting mazurkas, waltzes, polonnaises, nocturnes. Depressed by the fate of his dismembered fatherland, he wished to quicken compassion for Poland through music precisely as Mickiewicz was doing in poetry. When their country was resurrected at the close of the First World War, these geniuses, who had done so much to shape the cultural image of Poland in western Europe, were rewarded with handsome statues in Polish cities.

As an art form, music had been only slightly developed in Russia before 1800, save for religious chants which were cultivated by Orthodox churchmen. Native composers benefited from the patriotic emotionalism that was aroused by the desperate contest with Bonaparte. The first Russian musician to gain European reputation, Michael I. Glinka (1803–1857) was trained abroad, particularly in Italy. Yet in his compositions he sharply modified western fashions to fit the environment of the East and he skillfully merged popular Russian folk tunes with bewitching melodies, as was exemplified in the opera *A Life for the Tsar*. Honored as the founder of the national school of

music, Glinka heralded the coming of a truly great set
of Russian composers later in the century.

The Large Picture

After the convulsions of the French Revolution and
Napoleon, it is not surprising that there should have
been a reaction against the principles which underlay
the tumult and attendant agonies of heart and mind.
Religious conservatism worked hand in glove with
political conservatism to restore as much as possible of
the heritage of the past. Yet ideals of human freedom
and aspirations to national unity would not be denied.
In the humanities, in the things of the mind and the
spirit, an older classicism competing with a newer
romanticism resulted in the temporary triumph of the
latter. But the heyday of romanticism was over by
mid-century; realism was crowding to the fore in literature and impressionism in painting.

Space limitations have precluded consideration of
the advances in science and medicine, for example, in
the Age of Metternich; yet the creative and imaginative contributions of acknowledged masters in several
phases of the higher living have been touched upon.
Calling the roll of the gigantic personalities—Chateaubriand and Schleiermacher, Hegel and Baur in religious and philosophical thought; Lamartine, Goethe,
Heine, Pushkin, Mickiewicz in poetry; Dumas the elder,
Scribe, Grillparzer in drama; Hugo, Manzoni, George
Sand, Balzac, Gogol in the art of the novel; Michelet
and von Ranke in the writing of history; Delacroix,
Schwanthaler, Thorwaldsen in the fine arts; Schinkel,
von Klenze, de Montferrand in architecture; Beethoven, Schubert, Wagner, Berlioz, Verdi, Glinka
in musical composition—calling this roll makes it
understandable why the forepart of the nineteenth
century has been hailed as "the second Renaissance."

Bibliographical Note

"A book is the plectrum," mused Henry David Thoreau, "by which our else silent lyres are struck." Books here recommended have been chosen, for the most part, because of their sound scholarship, their perceptive interpretations, and their readability.

The most helpful gateway to works treating aspects of the Age of Metternich in depth are the relevant sections of *Guide to Historical Literature* (new ed., New York, 1961). A meritorius, though uneven, synthesis is John P. T. Bury, Ed., *The Zenith of Europe Power* (Cambridge, Eng., 1961). Much fuller on politics and diplomacy are the first four volumes of *Geschichte Europas seit den Verträgen von 1815 bis zum Frankfurter Frieden von 1871* (Stuttgart, 1894–1905) by Alfred Stern. Stressing materialism and class factors is Eric J. Hobshawn, *The Age of Revolution* (Cleveland, 1962); Metternich, grotesquely, is almost ignored. Better balanced and more effectively organized is Pierre Renouvin, *Le XIXᵉ Siècle*, vol. *I.*, *L'Europe des Nationalités et l'Éveil de Nouveaux Mondes* (2 vols., Paris, 1954–1955), by a master craftsman.

Carlton J. H. Hayes, *The Historical Evolution of Modern Nationalism* (new ed., New York, 1955) is clear in thought and vigorous in expression. Sturdy attempts to nail down that semantic something called liberalism have been made by Guido de Ruggiero, *The History of European Liberalism* (Eng. trans., new ed., London, 1959), which is much praised and much prized, and William A. Orton, *The Liberal Tradition* (New Haven, 1945). Basic works on general social and economic matters are Henri E. Seé, *Modern Capitalism* (Eng. trans., New York, 1928), offering a good over-all view; William O. Henderson, *The Industrial Revolution on the Continent* (Chicago, 1961), designedly an introduction; Herbert Heaton, *Economic History of Europe* (new ed., New York, 1948); Charles Gide and Charles Rist, *A History of Economic Doctrines* (Eng. trans., new ed., Boston, 1948), popular on both sides of the Atlantic; and Jürgen Kuczinski, *Labour Conditions in Western Europe* (New York, 1937). Egon C. Corti vividly recounts *The Rise of the House of Rothschild* (Eng. trans., New York, 1928).

Among stimulating collections of translated original materials are Jonathan F. Scott and Alexander Baltzly, Eds., *Readings in European History since 1814* (New York, 1930), and the first volume of *Europe in the Nineteenth Century* (Indianapolis, 1961), edited by Eugene N. Anderson and others.

CHAPTER 1

Unattractively written, though founded upon exhaustive investigations, is Heinrich von Srbik's *Metternich* (3 vols., Munich, 1925, 1954), which illuminates every facet of the chancellor's policy and personality. This monumental work forced modification in the "liberal" image of the prince, for he comes off as a diplomatic virtuoso of front rank, adept at calculating the future with skill and accuracy. The Srbik biography has been drawn upon by Helene du Coudray in *Metternich* (New Haven, 1936), which extols the man for timeless conservative principles, and by Bertier de Savigny in *Metternich et son Temps* (Paris, 1959). Superb essays on Metternich, Guizot, and the Roman Catholic Church may be found in Ernest L. Woodward, *Three Studies in Conservatism* (London, 1929). Available in an inadequate English translation (New York, 1880–1882) are five volumes of Metternich's personal papers *Aus Metternich's nachgelassenen Papieren* (8 vols., Vienna, 1880–1884), which must be studied critically. On Talleyrand, see a biography by Louis Madelin (Eng. trans., New York, 1948). Valuable insights into Russian world policy are furnished by Andrei Lobanov-Rostovsky, *Russia and Europe, 1789–1825* (Durham, 1947).

For the Vienna settlements, consult Harold Nicolson, *The Congress of Vienna* (New York, 1946), a literary master-piece; and Karl Griewank, *Der Wiener Kongress und die Neuordnung Europas* (Leipzig, 1942), which suffers from the Nazi environment in which it was composed. A realistic por-trait of a big, little man at Vienna is painted by Golo Mann in *Secretary of Europe: Friedrich von Gentz* (Eng. trans., new ed., New Haven, 1957). British diplomacy is authorita-tively reconstructed by Charles K. Webster, *The Foreign Policy of Castlereagh* (new ed., London, 1931), and by Harold W. V. Temperley, *The Foreign Policy of Canning* (London, 1925).

For the adventure in European cooperation after 1815: Paul W. Schroeder, *Metternich's Diplomacy at its Zenith* (Austin, Texas, 1962) combines minute research with hard thinking; also Henry W. Kissinger, *A World Restored* (Boston, 1957), who has read Srbik to good purpose; and *The Aftermath of the Napoleonic Wars* (London, 1947) by Hans G. Schenk, wider in range than the preceding. Standard on the making and the reception of the Monroe declaration of 1823 is *The Monroe Doctrine* (Cambridge, 1927) by Dexter Perkins. Treaties with explanatory maps are conveniently available in Edward Hertslet, *The Map of Europe by Treaty,* vols. 1 and II (London, 1875).

CHAPTER 2

Excellent to start with on the aftermath of Napoleon is Frederick B. Artz, *Reaction and Revolution* (New York, 1934), an imaginative synthesis with discriminating bibli-ographical notes. The same scholar emphasizes non-political affairs in *France under the Bourbon Restoration* (Cam-bridge, 1931). Straightforward and sober is Félix Ponteil, *La*

Monarchie Parlamentaire (Paris, 1949). Sébastien C. G. Charléty, *La Restauration* (Paris, 1921) colorfully recaptures the spirit of its theme. The short *Revolutionary Movement in France* by John P. Plamenatz (New York, 1952) supersedes other titles on the subject. Lucid and authoritative is John H. Clapham, *The Economic Development of Germany and France* (new ed., Cambridge, Eng., 1936). French economic evolution is also carefully explained by Arthur L. Dunham in *The Industrial Revolution in France* (New York, 1955), and by Rondo E. Cameron in *France and the Economic Development of Europe* (Princeton, 1961), a trailblazing volume. On King Charles X, there is an informative biography (Paris, 1928) by Pierre de la Gorce; the Paris events of 1830 are graphically described in *La Révolution de 1830* (Paris, 1950) by Robert Demoulin.

Henry B. Clarke, *Modern Spain* (Cambridge, Eng., 1906) is reliable, but often a little dull because of its detail; Charles E. Nowell, *A History of Portugal* (New York, 1952) provides a fine introduction. Unfriendly to Roman Catholicism, Bolton King, *A History of Italian Unity* (2 vols., London, 1912) is thoroughgoing and has not been supplanted by the admirable first two volumes of *Italy in the Making* (3 vols., Cambridge, Eng., 1932, 1935, 1940) by George F. H. Berkeley, which has a slightly pro-Catholic accent. *The Bourbons of Naples* (London, 1956) by Harold Acton stresses personalities in a rich reading experience.

Franz Schnabel, *Deutsche Geschichte im neunzehnten Jahrhundert* (new ed., 4 vols., Freiburg im Breisgau, 1948–1951), of which the second and fourth volumes have relevance to the Age of Metternich, is a classic. History was made nearly as much as it was written by Heinrich G. von Treitschke, *History of Germany in the Nineteenth Century* (Eng. trans., 7 vols., New York, 1915–1919), eloquent and tantalizing and biased against Metternich. *La libéralisme Rhénan* (new ed., Paris, 1949) by Jacques Droz is a sensitive and meticulous survey. Judicious treatments of the intellectuals are Richard H. Thomas, *Liberalism, Nationalism, and the German Intellectuals* (Cambridge, Eng., 1951), and

Leonard Krieger, *The German Idea of Freedom* (Boston, 1957). High standards of scholarship distinguish Theodore S. Hamerow, *Restoration, Revolution, and Reaction in Germany* (Princeton, 1958). William O. Henderson, *The Zollverein* (new ed., London, 1959) is a masterly re-examination of the customs union.

For Eastern Europe: William Miller, *The Ottoman Empire and its Successors* (new ed., Cambridge, Eng., 1936), and Harold W. V. Temperley, *History of Serbia* (London, 1917), both needing not a little revision. Short and urbane is Christopher M. Woodhouse, *The Greek War of Independence* (London, 1952). Jerome Blum, *Lord and Peasant in Russia* (Princeton, 1962) is of absorbing interest and well balanced. Interesting and important biographies of Alexander I are Maurice Paléologue, *The Enigmatic Tsar* (London, 1938), and Leonid I. Strakovsky, *Alexander I of Russia* (New York, 1947); the latter examines the evidence on whether the emperor really died in 1825. On revolutionary currents, read Mikhail Zeitlin, *The Decembrists* (London, 1958), a fascinating narrative.

CHAPTER 3

As suggested by their titles, many of the books selected for Chapter II extend across the years 1830–1848. Admirers of the learning of William L. Langer patiently await the publication of his long-promised *Liberalism, Nationalism, and Socialism, 1832–1852*. Jacob S. Schapiro, *Liberalism and the Challenge of Fascism* (New York, 1949) is made up of painstaking, not entirely convincing essays. Sébastien C. G. Charléty, *La Monarchie de Juillet* (Paris, 1921) is a dispassionate exposition; Thomas E. B. Howarth, *The Citizen King* (London, 1961), a beautifully written life of Louis Philippe. John M. S. Allison, *Thiers and the French Monarchy* (New York, 1926) is a first-class piece of work on a complicated character. For his arch rival, the finest study is *Guizot* (London, 1963) by Douglas Johnson, a learned appraisal of policies and principles rather than conventional biography. The relevant portions of Guizot's *Mémoires pour Servir à Histoire de Mon Temps* (8 vols., 1858–1867) are suggestive. Data on the Napoleonic legend appear in *The Rise of Louis Napoleon* (new ed., London, 1951) by Frederick A. Simpson.

Authoritative on the creation of Belgium and British maneuvers in the Near East is Charles K. Webster, *The Foreign Policy of Palmerston* (2 vols., London, 1951). Mazzini comes to life in biographies by two staunch admirers, Gwilyn O. Griffith (London, 1932) and Gaetano Salvemini (Eng. trans., New York, 1957); the latter, which analyzes certain writings of the prophet, may appropriately be read in conjunction with Giuseppe Mazzini, *The Duties of Man* (Eng. trans., New York, 1907). Accuracy and breadth characterize Kent R. Greenfield, *Economics and Liberalism in the Risorgimento* (Baltimore, 1934), which sweeps the reader along in tracing Italian antipathy to Austrian dominance.

In addition to the books on German Europe previously recommended, Egon C. Corti, *Ludwig I. von Bayern* (new ed., Munich, 1960), impressionistic, and *The Life of Friederich List* (London, 1909) by Margaret E. Hirst may be mentioned.

For the Austrian empire, the best approach is Chapters XVII–XIX in the second volume of Hugo Hantsch, *Die Geschichte Österreichs* (new ed., 2 vols., Vienna, 1962), an encyclopedic synthesis. A much fuller account is provided in *Vormärz. Die Ära Metternich 1815 bis 1848* (Potsdam, 1948) by Werner Meyer. Rural affairs are definitively co-ordinated by Jerome Blum, *Noble Landowners and Agriculture in Austria* (Baltimore, 1948). Fragments of truth may be found in Alan J. P. Taylor, *The Habsburg Monarchy* (new ed., London, 1949). Otto Zarek, *Kossuth* (Eng. trans., London, 1937) is colorful, though less rewarding than it should be. Carlile A. Macartney, *Hungary* (Chicago, 1962) offers a brief panoramic survey.

For the empire of the tsars, a work of rare erudition and a Gargantuan meal, upon which western students rely, is

Theodor Schieman, *Geschichte Russlands unter Kaiser Nikolaus I* (4 vols., Berlin, 1904–1919); the first volume reconstructs the reign of Alexander I. Rather frothy, but with extensive quotations from archives is Constantin de Grunwald, *Tsar Nicholas I* (London, 1954). *The Third Section* (Cambridge, 1961) by Sidney Monas is the most competent study on the subject. And the same appraisal holds for R. F. Leslie, *Polish Politics and the Revolution of 1830* (London, 1956) .

Two foreigners who traveled widely in Russia, the first a French aristocrat, the other an experienced German investigator, prepared permanently useful accounts of their observations: Marquis de Astolphe L. L. Custine, *Journey for Our Time* (Eng. trans., New York, 1951), and August von Hauxthausen, *The Russian Empire, its People, Institutions, and Resources* (abridged Eng. trans., London, 1856). For intellectual currents, see a sterling book by a Czech professor and statesman, Thomas G. Masaryk, *The Spirit of Russia* (2 vols., new ed., New York, 1955), sketchy on the early nineteenth century; and Hans Kohn, *Pan Slavism, its History and Ideology* (Notre Dame, 1953), delightful and learned. Regarding Petr I. Liashchenko, *History of the National Economy of Russia* (Eng. trans., New York, 1949), the several editions in the original language illustrate the shifting tides in Soviet interpretation of the past.

To understand the amazing and audacious Mehemet Ali, read Henry H. Dodwell, *The Founder of Modern Egypt, Muhammed Ali* (Cambridge, Eng., 1931). François Charles-Roux, *Thiers et Méhémet-Ali* (Paris, 1951) capably untangles the mercurial diplomacy of France. Pertinent and revealing is John H. Gleason, *The Genesis of Russophobia in Great Britain* (Cambridge, 1950) .

French social thought and terrestrial Utopias are summarized by George D. H. Cole, *A History of Socialist Thought,* vol. I (London, 1953), and set out in rich detail in these books: David O. Evans, *Social Romanticism in France* (Eng. trans., Oxford, 1951); Frank E. Manuel, *The New World of Henri St. Simon* (Cambridge, 1956) ; George

Woodcock, *Pierre-Joseph Proudhon* (London, 1956). For a crisp, fresh and intelligent introduction to Karl Marx, a biography by Isaiah Berlin (new ed., New York, 1959) will do very well.

CHAPTER 4

Christianity in a Revolutionary Age, vols. I and II (New York, 1958) by Kenneth S. Latourette is a massive work, though not easy to read. Edward E. Y. Hales, *The Catholic Church in the Modern World* (New York, 1958) is a meaningful integration by a Catholic scholar. Charles S. Phillips, *The Church in France,* vol. I (2 vols., New York, 1929, 1936) provides a full and most interesting narrative. Béla Menczer, *Catholic Political Thought* (London, 1952) is a not particularly critical re-examination. Much more specialized are Francis Bayle, *Les Idées Politiques de Joseph de Maistre* (Paris, 1945); Jean B. Duroselle, *Les débuts du Catholicisme Social en France* (Paris, 1951); and René Rémond, *Lamennais* (Paris, 1948), the last exceptionally fine reading.

Theological interests in Protestant Europe are compactly recounted in Edward C. Moore, *An Outline of the History of Christian Thought since Kant* (New York, 1912). *A History of Free Thought in the Nineteenth Century,* vol. I (2 vols., New York, 1930) by John M. Robertson throws brilliant light on many facets of developments in religion, as does John S. Curtiss, *Church and State in Russia* (New York, 1940). Sergei N. Bulgakov, *The Orthodox Church* (Eng. trans., London, 1935) deals with its theme in broad perspective; unfailing grasp of essentials is shown in *The Jewish Fate and Future* (London, 1940) by Arthur Ruppin.

It is improbable that Georg M. C. Brandes, *Main Currents in Nineteenth-Century Literature* (6 vols., New York, 1901–1905), will soon be relegated to the back shelves. For French literary contributions, Maurice A. Souriau, *Histoire de romantisme en France* (3 vols., Paris, 1927–1928) is sufficiently detailed to appease the most voracious appetite; also,

Albert J. George, *The Development of French Romanticism* (Syracuse, 1953), and André Maurois, *Olympio: The Life of Victor Hugo* (Eng. trans., New York, 1956) are substantial achievements, the latter gayer reading than its companion.

If Ludwig W. Kahn, *Social Ideals in German Literature* (New York, 1938) fails to satisfy tastes adequately, turn to the stiff presentation in Rudolf Haym, *Die Romantische Schule* (new ed., Berlin, 1928). Dmitrii S. Mirsky, *A History of Russian Literature* (new ed., New York, 1934); Ernest J. Simmons, *Pushkin* (Cambridge, 1937); John Mersereaux, Jr., *Mikhail Lermontov* (Carbondale, Ill., 1962); and Julian Krzyzanowski, *Polish Romantic Literature* (New York, 1931) —all open Slavic doors.

For its subject matter, nothing approaches George P. Gooch, *History and Historians in the Nineteenth Century* (new ed., London, 1952), invaluable for students of history and infectious as literature.

Julius Meier-Graefe, *Modern Art* (Eng. trans., 2 vols., New York, 1908), despite its age, still ranks at or near the top of comprehensive books on the fine arts. Other clear and interesting manuals are Thomas Craven, *Modern Art* (New York, 1934), and Fritz Novotny, *Painting and Sculpture in Europe* (Baltimore, 1960). Luc Benoist, *La Sculpture Française* (Paris, 1945) unites erudition with readability. *Architecture* (Baltimore, 1958) by Henry R. Hitchcock is more solid and harder to follow than Nikolaus L. B. Pevsner, *An Outline of European Architecture* (new ed., Baltimore, 1960).

Music in the Romantic Era (London, 1947) by Alfred Einstein is a highly creditable performance, as is his *Schubert* (London, 1951). The towering genius of Beethoven is depicted in an unpretentious biography by Marion N. Scott (New York, 1934). Donald J. Grout, *A Short History of Opera* (New York, 1947), in spite of its brevity, stands up well. Truly remarkable for re-creation of the atmosphere of the time is Jacques Barzun, *Berlioz and His Century* (new ed., New York, 1956). Gaps that remain may be filled in by recourse to Ludwig Schiedermaier, *Einführung in das Studium der Musikgeschichte* (new ed., Bonn, 1947).

Index

Adrianople, treaty of, 50, 51
Aix-la-Chapelle, congress of, 20–21
Albanians, 45
Alexander I, of Russia, 9–12, 16, 19, 23–24, 54–57, 115, 134
Algeria, 62, 65, 66
Alsace-Lorraine, 13
Andersen, Hans C., 124
Anglo-Austro-French treaty (1815), 11
Anticapitalism, 99–103
Aracheev, Aleksei, 57
Architecture, 132–135
Arndt, Ernst M., 42
Association for the Propagation of the Faith, 108
Auber, Daniel F., 137–138
Austria, and Congress of Vienna, 14, 16; and the Germanies, 15, 44; and Italy, 21, 34, 38, 72, 121; and the Balkans, 48, 49; realm and peoples of, 78–85; end of Metternich era in, 85–87
Baden, 40
Balkan Peninsula (the Near East), 23, 76, 94–96, 116–117
Balzac, Honoré, 67, 125–126
Baur, Ferdinand C., 114
Bavaria, 15, 40, 73, 77
Beethoven, Ludwig van, 135–136
Belgium, and Congress of Vienna, 14, 17; independence movement in, 68–69
Berlin, 41
Berlioz, Hector, 137–138
Bernadotte, Marshal, 17
Bessarabia, 16
Biblical criticism, 113–114
Bismarck, Otto von, 77
Blanc, Louis, 101–102
Bonald, Louis de, 109
Bonapartism, 28–29, 61, 66, 102
Bosio, François, 131
Bourgeoisie, 30, 34, 37, 39, 40, 63, 73, 77, 81, 84, 86

Brazil, 32
Brussels, 68
Bulgars, 45, 51, 116, 117
Burschenschaften, 42–43
Cabet, Étienne, 101
Calvinism, 111, 112
Canning, George, 23, 24
Canova, Antonio, 132
Cape of Good Hope, 17
Carbonari, 37–39, 69
Carlsbad Decrees, 43–44, 73
Castlereagh, Lord, 9, 11, 14, 16, 19, 21, 23, 35
Ceylon, 17
Chamisso, Adelbert von, 124
Charles X, of France (comte d'Artois), 28, 60–62
Charter of 1814, French, 6, 7, 65
Chateaubriand, François, 108, 119
Chopin, Frédéric F., 138
Consalvi, Ercole, 35
Constantine, grand duke, 59
Cornelius, Peter von, 131
Corot, Camille, 130
Cortot, Jean P., 131
Cracow, 16, 84–85
Croats, 81
Czechs, 81, 85, 131
Dalmatia, 14
Danzig (Gdansk), 14
Daumier, Honoré, 130
Decembrist revolt, 58–60, 122
Delacroix, Eugène, 129–130
Denmark, 17
Don Carlos, of Portugal, 31–32
Dresden, 39, 41, 134, 137
Dukobors, 116
Dumas, Alexandre, the elder, 122–123, 124
Dutch Netherlands, see Netherlands, kingdom of
Egypt, 95, 96
Eliot, George, 114
Emerson, Ralph Waldo, 1, 101
England, see Great Britain

Ferdinand I, of Austria, 86
Ferdinand I, of the Two Sicilies, 22, 38
Ferdinand VII, of Spain, 20, 23, 30, 31
Fine Arts, 129–132
Finland, 16, 53
Florence, 35
Fourier, François, 100–101
France, the peace treaties of 1814–1815 and, 6–7, 13, 19; under the Bourbon Restoration, 6–7, 27–30, 60–62; under the July Monarchy, 64–68, 96, 97–98, 103–104. *See* Charter of 1814, French; Fine Arts; French literature.
Francis I, of Austria, 78, 79, 96
Frederick William III, of Prussia, 9, 75
Frederick William IV, of Prussia, 76, 77, 133
Freeman, Edward, 106
French literature, 119–120, 122–123, 124, 125–126
Galicia, 16, 84, 85, 107
Garibaldi, Giuseppe, 71
Genoa, 16
Gentz, Friedrich von, 9, 43
Géricault, Jean L., 129, 130
German literature, 120–121, 123, 124, 125
Germanic Confederation, 15–16
Germany (the Germanies), Congress of Vienna and, 14–16; evolution of, 39–45, 72–78. *See* Prussia; Fine Arts; German literature.
Gioberti, Vincenzo, 71
Glinka, Michael I., 138–139
Goethe, Johann W. von, 41, 120
Gogol, Nikolai, 123–124, 125
Great Britain, Congress of Vienna and, 9, 17–18; and the congress period, 20, 21–22, 23, 24; and Greece, 48–49; and Belgian independence, 69
Greece, 23, 45, 47–51, 116–117
Grillparzer, Franz, 123
Grün, Anastasius, 120–121
Guizot, François P. G., 66–67, 97, 103–104, 112, 126–127

Hanover, 73
Hapsburg, *see* Austria
Hardenberg, Prince Karl A. von, 9
Haydn, Josef, 135
Hegel, George W. F., 99, 113
Heine, Heinrich, 77, 120, 137
Heligoland, 17
Herzen, Alexander, 60, 99
Hetairia Philiké, 48
Holy Alliance, the, 19, 115
Hugo, Victor, 60, 109, 119, 120, 123, 137
Hundred Days, the, 12–13
Hungarians (Magyars), 81–83
Ingres, Jean A., 129
Ionian Islands, 17
Isabella II, of Spain, 31, 32
Italian literature, 121, 124
Italy, and Congress of Vienna, 16–17; liberalism and reaction in, 33–39, 69–72, 83–84. *See* Fine Arts; Italian literature.
Ivanov, Alexander, 131
Jahn, Friedrich L., 41–42
Janissaries, the, 45, 46, 49
Jesuits, the, 28, 31, 107, 115
Jews, the, 53, 86, 117–118
John VI, of Portugal, 32
July ordinances, 62
Junkers, 40
Karageorge, 46, 47
Karamzin, Nicholas, 127
Klenze, Franz von, 133, 134
Kollár, Jan, 122
Kolowrat, Francis A., 79, 86
Kossuth, Louis, 82, 83, 87, 111
Kotzebue, August F. F., 43, 56
Lafayette, Marquis Marie J., 61, 62
Laibach (Ljubljana), congress of, 22
Lamartine, Alphonse de, 119
Lamennais, Félicité de, 109–110
Lanner, Josef, 136
Lelewel, Joachim, 128
Leopardi, Giacomo, 121
Leopold I, of Belgium, 69
Lermontov, Mikhail, 122
Liberals (Liberalism), 3, 30, 76, 78, 82

List, Friedrich, 74, 82
Lombardy, 14, 16, 34, 83, 124
Louis XVIII, of France, 6, 10, 12, 13, 27–28, 30
Louis Napoleon, 98
Louis Philippe, of France, 32, 62, 64–68, 97–98, 104, 110, 130, 134
Ludwig I, of Bavaria, 131, 133, 134
Lutheranism, 111–112
Luxemburg, 15
Lyons, 68, 108
Maistre, Joseph de, 108–109
Malta, 17
Manzoni, Alessandro, 121, 124
Marx, Karl, 1, 75, 99, 103, 118
Mazzini, Giuseppe, 70–71
Mehemet Ali, 49, 95, 96, 97, 100
Metternich, Prince Clemens, his place in history, 1–3; his ideas and character, 3–5, 80, 121; and the peace settlements of 1814–1815, 8–9, 10, 16, 19; and the congress period, 20, 21, 22–26; and Italy, 21–22, 36, 38, 72; and central Europe, 43, 73, 78–87; and the Balkans, 48, 49, 50, 94, 95–96; and Russia, 55, 56, 59, 94, 95–96; flight from Vienna, 87, 104
Meyerbeer, Giacomo, 138
Michelet, Jules, 126
Mickiewicz, Adam, 122, 138
Milan, 34, 37, 39, 84
Monroe Doctrine, 24–25
Montalembert, comte Charles de, 110
Montferrand, August R. de, 135
Moscow, 54, 58, 91, 93
Mozart, Wolfgang A., 135
Münchengrätz, 96
Munich, 39, 40, 41, 131–132, 133–134
Music, 135–139
Musset, Alfred de, 120
Naples, 36, 38
Napoleon, 2, 5, 8, 10, 12–13, 18, 27, 29, 33, 98, 107, 117, 121, 131, 137
Navarino Bay, 49–50

Neo-Holy Alliance, 21–22
Netherlands, kingdom of, 15, 17, 68–69
Ney, Michel, 12, 28–29
Nicholas I, of Russia, 59, 64, 87–94, 96, 111, 115, 134
Norway, 17
Obrenovich, Milosh, 46, 47
Otto, of Greece, 50
Orléans, duke of, see Louis Philippe, of France
Orthodox Eastern Church, 45, 53, 92, 114–117
Ottoman Empire (Turkey), 16, 45–51, 94–96
Ozanam, Antoine F., 110
Palacky, Frantisek, 85, 128
Panizzi, Anthony, 39
Papacy, the 35, 36. See States of the Church.
Paris, first Treaty of (1814), 6
Paris, second Treaty of (1815), 13
Pestel, Paul I., 58, 59
Philhellenism, 47, 49
Piedmont, see Sardinia
Pius IX, 72, 84
Poland (and Poles), 10, 11, 14, 16, 53, 56, 81, 84–85, 88–91, 111, 122, 131, 138. See Galicia.
Polignac, prince Jules de, 61
Portugal, 17, 32–33
Pradier, James, 131
Press, 35, 66, 82
Protestantism, 111–113
Proudhon, Pierre J., 102–103
Prussia, and Congress of Vienna, 9, 11, 14–15; liberalism and reaction in, 40, 75–76; and *Zollverein*, 44, 73
Pushkin, Alexander, 55, 89, 121–122
Quadruple Alliance, 19–20
Quintuple Alliance, 20–21
Railways, 67, 72, 74, 84, 86, 93–94
Ranke, Leopold von, 128
Raskolniki, 116
Rauch, Christian, 132
Rietschel, Ernst F., 132
Roman Catholic Church, 7, 28, 35, 53, 78, 89, 106–111
Romanticism, analyzed, 118–119
Rossi, Karl I., 134

Rossini, Gioachino, 137
Rothschild, 5, 67, 79, 118
Rousseau, Théodore, 130
Rude, François, 131
Ruhr, 15, 74
Rumanians, 45, 51, 116, 117
Russia, and Congress of Vienna, 9, 10, 11, 16; and the congress period, 20, 23, 24; and the Balkans, 46, 49, 50–51, 95; and the Poles, 10, 11, 14, 16, 56, 88–91, 111; social structure of, 51–55; under Alexander I, 55–57; Decembrist rising, 58–60; under Nicholas I, 87–94. *See* Fine Arts; Orthodox Eastern Church.
Russian Literature, 91–92, 121–122, 123, 124, 125
Ruthenians, *see* Ukrainians
Saar Valley, 13, 15
Saint-Simon, comte Henri de, 99–100
Sand, George, 125
Sand, Karl, 43
Sardinia, kingdom of (Piedmont), 16, 37, 39
Saxony, 11, 14, 15, 77
Schinkel, Karl F. von, 133
Schleiermacher, Friedrich D., 112–113
Schubert, Franz, 136
Schumann, Robert A., 137
Schwanthaler, Ludwig von, 132
Scott, Sir Walter, 124
Scribe, Eugène, 123
Secret societies, 30, 37, 38, 48, 58, 89
Sedlnitzky, Josef, 78
Serbia, 45, 46–47, 116, 117
Slave trade, 18
Slavic literature, 121–122
Slavophiles, 92, 115
Slovaks, 81, 82
Society of Jesus, *see* Jesuits
Spain, 17, 20, 23, 24, 30–31, 97
Spanish colonies, 23, 24, 31
St. Petersburg (Leningrad), 23, 54, 58, 93, 134
States of the Church (Papal States), 16, 35, 36, 69, 72
Stendhal (Henri Beyle), 125

Storm, Theodor, 125
Strauss, David F., 114
Strauss, Johann, the elder, 136
Sweden, 16, 17
Switzerland, 17
Széchenyi, Stephen, 82, 83
Talleyrand, prince Charles M. de, 10, 11, 78
Thiers, Adolphe, 66, 96, 127
"Third section," 88, 91
Thorwaldsen, Bertel, 132
Tocqueville, Alexis de, 98
Tolstoy, Count Leo, 53
Triple Alliance (1815), 11
Troppau (Opava), conference of, 21, 22
Turkey, *see* Ottoman Empire
Turkish Straits, 53, 94, 96
Tuscany, 16, 34
Two Sicilies, kingdom of the, 16, 21, 22, 36–38, 72
Tyrol, 15
Ukrainians, 16, 53, 84–85, 124
Ultramontanism, 107
Uniate Catholics, 53, 111
United States of America, 12, 24–25, 39, 90
Universities, 41, 73, 91
Unkiar Skelessi, treaty of, 95
Utopian socialists, 99–101
Uvarov, S. S., 91
Venetia, 14, 16, 23, 83
Verdi, Giuseppe, 137
Verona, congress of, 23
Vienna, 45, 80, 85, 86, 87, 107, 117, 120, 121, 123, 132, 134, 135, 136
Vienna, Congress and treaty of, 7–18
Vigny, Alfred de, 119
Voltaire, François Marie, 52, 110
Wagner, Richard, 137
Waldmüller, Ferdinand G., 131
Warsaw, 89, 90
Wartburg, 42
Waterloo, 12
Weber, Carl M. von, 136–137
Wellington, Duke of, 4, 9, 50
Württemberg, 40
Young Germany, 120
Young Italy, 70, 71, 83
Zollverein, 44, 73